CW00544534

SALT CRYSTALS ON AN AXE

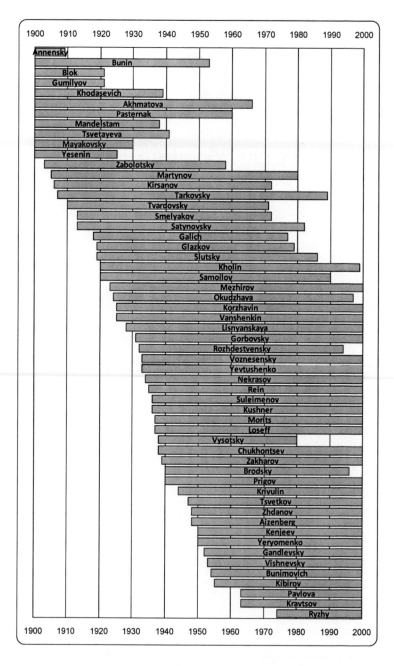

Authors' lifetimes within the limits of the 20th century

Salt Crystals on an Axe

Twentieth-Century Russian Poetry in Congruent Translation

A Bilingual Mini-Anthology

Compiled and edited by S. Muchnick

Translated by A. Shafarenko

ancient
purple

Published by Ancient Purple Translations

Original poems © individual copyright holders (see the list on p. xiii)
This collection © Ancient Purple 2009
English translations © Alex Shafarenko 2009
Notes and Editor's Introduction © Slava Muchnick 2009

No part of this book may be reproduced or stored in a retrieval
system without prior written permission of the copyright holders

ISBN 978-0-9563075-1-4

Printed and bound by Lightning Source
in La Vergne, TN, USA and Milton Keynes, England

Ancient Purple
Pump House, Quarry Road
Godalming, Surrey GU7 2RW
England

www.ancientpurple.com

To the memory of Paul Sherlock

CONTENTS

Through the pallid window pane

The catalogue of ships

A red-chested bullfinch

To see this day

The one who wakes

The same old heaven

Appendix

PREFACE

What does this book offer?

- All-new translations which consistently preserve the poetic form of the originals. Metre and rhyme continue to be at the core of Russian poetry – for its authors as much as for its discerning readership.
- Short to very short poems, ideally suited for memorising, reciting and quoting from memory.
- A panoramic view covering not only the universally acknowledged masters but also many other poets who left their unmistakable mark on the poetic legacy of the 20th century. Each author is represented by two poems.
- All in all, a compact introduction into the fascinating portable world of small-form poetry that is carried along by every cultured speaker of Russian, and which can now be glimpsed through the medium of English.

Who is it for?

- English-language poetry aficionados who are not averse to the new and the unusual. We offer them an opportunity to appreciate Russian poetry on its own terms, complete with its characteristic formal features, which is a very different experience from reading "domesticated" translations.
- Students of Russian who wish to get to grips with the poetic language and form, and to understand the differences between English and Russian poetic traditions (the 20th century is the best starting point for this). Indexes of metres and rhyme schemes found in the Appendix help the reader to find examples of a particular form. The presence of congruent translations alongside the originals makes the texts accessible as works of art rather than mere literary artefacts even to beginners whose knowledge of the language is modest.

- The members of the Russian diaspora who have always wanted to share works of their favourite poets with their English-speaking friends, but who could not find translations with which they would agree.
- Translators and linguists interested in the theory and practice of verse translation.
- Youngsters of English-Russian bilingual upbringing whose command of Russian falls short of the necessary standard for appreciating poetry in the original.

What else is there?
- Editor's introduction describing and justifying the system of congruent translation which has been consistently applied throughout this Anthology.
- Annotations to both the translations and the originals.
- A concise timeline of 20th-century Russian history putting the poems in context.

Acknowledgements

The following authors and copyright holders kindly granted their permission to reproduce original Russian poems and to publish English translations: Mikhail Aizenberg; Margarita Novgorodova (for the works of Anna Akhmatova and Nikolai Gumilyov); the Estate of Joseph Brodsky; Evgeny Bunimovich; Oleg Chukhontsev; Alexandra Galich (for Alexander Galich); Sergey Gandlevsky; Nikolai Glazkov, Jr. (for Nikolai Glazkov); Gleb Gorbovsky; Bakhyt Kenjeev; Arina Kholina (for Igor Kholin); Timur Kibirov; Olga Khazova (for Semyon Kirsanov); Naum Korzhavin; Konstantin Kravtsov; Olga Kushlina (for Victor Krivulin); Alexander Kushner; Inna Lisnyanskaya; Lev Loseff; Galina Sukhova (for Leonid Martynov); Alexander Mezhirov; Yunna Morits; Vsevolod Nekrasov; Olga Artsimovich (for Bulat Okudzhava); Henrich Neigaus, Marina Neigaus, Elena Pasternak, Evgeny Pasternak and Natalia Pasternak (for Boris Pasternak); Vera Pavlova; Nadezhda Bourova (for Dmitri A. Prigov); Evgeny Rein; Alla Kireeva (for Robert Rozhdestvensky); Irina Knyazeva (for Boris Ryzhy); Alexander Davydov, Pavel Kaufman and Galina Medvedeva (for David Samoilov); Victoria Pashkovskaya (for Jan Satunovsky); Olga Frizen (for Boris Slutsky); Olzhas Suleimenov; Dmitry Studenetsky, Marina Tarkovskaya and Arseny Tarkovsky, Jr (for Arseny Tarkovsky); Alexei Tsvetkov; Olga Tvardovskaya and Valentina Tvardovskaya (for Alexander Tvardovsky); Konstantin Vanshenkin; Vladimir Vishnevsky; Andrey Voznesensky; Arkady Vysotsky, Nikita Vysotsky and Marina de Poliakoff (for Vladimir Vysotsky); Alexander Yeremenko; Yevgeny Yevtushenko; Nikita Zabolotsky (for Nikolai Zabolotsky); Vladimir Zakharov; Ivan Zhdanov.

Gregory Falkovich provided a sympathetic ear when the vague ideas that eventually led to this book were first aired. His vision of its potential audience and his input into the discussions about some of the originals helped us and cheered us up. Timothy Steele's thoughtful criticism of sample translations was invaluable and allowed us to clear a potentially damaging confusion; his encouragement at a difficult stage meant a lot to us. Barry Scherr read the manuscript when it was nearing completion and provided most helpful comments. He also kindly sent us a copy of his out-of-print monograph on Russian prosody.

We were blessed with a panel of English colleagues and friends who took it upon themselves to read, and take apart, draft translations. Paul Sherlock's enthusiasm, love of poetry, vast knowledge, broad-mindedness and sense of humour were a massive asset for the project; his criticism and suggestions have been taken onboard in many cases. Chris Jesshope read dozens of draft translations and provided strong opinions which lead to important improvements and were very stimulating. Michael Bartholomew-Biggs, Daniel Gilberthorpe, Steve Hunt, Tristan Millington-Drake and Vladimir Moss checked many translations and came up with valuable suggestions. Matthew Armstrong, Judith Bailey, and Clive and Jane Carter read some of the drafts and made useful comments. It should be stated in the strongest possible terms that none of the panellists is in any way responsible for any mistakes, clumsiness, lack of artistry etc. in the translations included in the Anthology. Any such transgressions are ours and ours alone, as we did resist proposed changes on many occasions.

Galina Muchnick and Vladimir Zakharov discussed the selection of authors with us and suggested some of the works included in the anthology. Igor Loshchilov provided important insight into one of the poems by Zabolotsky. Alexey Kudryavtsev helped us to verify the history timeline found in the Appendix.

Ivan Ahmetyev, Vitaly Beloborodtsev, Olga Ermolaeva, Mikhail Etelzon, Alexei Grinbaum, Alexander Izbitser, Anatoly Kudryavitsky, Victor Kulle, Alexander Kushner, Dmitry Kuzmin, Natalia Osipova, David Patashinsky, Nina Perova, Dmitry Polischuk, Nadezhda Rein, Larisa Spiridonova, the Russian Authors' Society, the Russian PEN Centre and the *Znamya* magazine assisted with contacting copyright holders. The FTM agency and the Subsidiary Rights department of Farrar, Straus and Giroux have been very helpful with arranging permissions for the works of the authors represented by them. Alexandra Belitskaya handled the legal matters related to Vladimir Vysotsky's copyright.

NOTE ON PRESENTATION

The use of British English and US English in translations and the approach to punctuation and capitalisation are explained on p. xlviii. The policy with respect to additional information is summarised on p. li.

Many of the works in the book are untitled, which is common in Russian poetry, especially for shorter pieces. Such poems are traditionally printed with asterisks in place of the title and are referred to by their first line. We have followed this convention in the presentation of untitled poems in both languages.

The names of the authors and of the people mentioned in dedications or annotations are, as a rule, given in their established English spelling. This has been done even at the expense of consistency: for example, Okud**zh**ava but Ken**j**eev (both spelled with ж in Russian), **Ye**vgeny Yevtushenko but **E**vgeny Rein. When the way in which the name was spelled in English-language publications had changed over the years, we used the most recent known version.

Unattributed poetic translations in the Introduction and annotations are by A. Shafarenko. Biblical references are to the King James Version and the 1876 Synodal Translation [into Russian] unless otherwise specified.

To make the originals more accessible to the readers whose command of Russian is less than perfect, we indicate the position of word stress where it may be ambiguous, where a non-normative stress was intended by the author, and also in rare proper names; we use the letter ë wherever there is even the slightest chance of the e/ë ambiguity. When transliterated Russian words occur in translation (which mainly happens with proper names), we mark the stress with accented vowels.

SYMBOLS

When discussing general metrical patterns, we use the classical scansion symbols – the notation which is standard for Russian prosody and is sometimes employed in English too:

∪	Weak (metrically unstressed) syllable.
–	Strong syllable: stressed in English; tends to be stressed in Russian.
‖	Caesura.

The following symbols are used when discussing the distribution of actual stresses in the Russian originals:

∪	Unstressed syllable.
´	Stressed syllable.
˝	Syllable carrying both a lexical and a phrasal stress.

Rhyme schemes are described using the following notation:

a b …	Verse lines forming masculine rhymes: *a* rhymes with *a*, *b* with *b* etc. Typographic lines do not always coincide with verse lines.
A B …	Lines forming feminine rhymes.
A' B' …	Lines forming dactylic or longer rhymes.
α β …	Rhymed lines that switch between masculine, feminine etc. while occupying a fixed position within a stable rhyme pattern.
x X X'	Unrhymed lines of the respective ending type.

Editor's Introduction

"Twentieth-century Russian poetry" and "contemporary Russian poetry" are no longer the same thing. The passage of time has made it possible to see the poetic output of the 20th century for what it is: a towering collective achievement, firmly rooted in the legacy of what is known as the Golden Age of Russian poetry; an achievement which can readily be judged by the standards of that era, and which arguably even makes the poetry of the Golden Age look, in a sense, one-dimensional. Naturally, all of this only becomes apparent after some sieving, but given the circumstances of the time and place, it is surprising how little needs to be discarded.

For all the diversity of 20th-century Russian poetry, there is a strong sense of unity about it which makes it a clear-cut literary period – distinct from, though intimately linked with, what happened before and what is happening now. We have tried to reflect both that diversity and that unity in the present Anthology. We also set out to preserve the poetic form in translation; in our view, which will be outlined in the rest of the Introduction, it would be impossible to do justice to the poetry of this period otherwise. Each poem is rendered in English keeping to the metre and rhyme scheme of the Russian original on the facing page. All translation has been done by the same translator, who has consistently adhered to a set of principles in rendering individual poems selected for the book.

With 56 authors included, the Anthology reflects the main trends, styles and themes of the Russian 20th century. It also amounts to a medium-scale experiment in congruent translation: as evidenced by the index on p. 368, all primary Russian metrical schemes are covered, as are logaoedics, imitative classical verse, *dolnik* and accentual verse; the reader will even find an instance of sporadic syllabic verse. The rhyme schemes (see p. 369) range from no rhyme at all to the French sonnet to special arrangements which stretch even the very rhymable Russian language.

What's in a Form?

Russian poetry of the 20th century is generally metrical and usually rhymed, and in this respect it stands in sharp contrast to the English poetic tradition of the same period. Moreover, the role of form in mainstream Russian poetry is critically important: it often carries as much of the overall message of the poem as its verbal substance. Not only are metre and rhyme aesthetically pleasing, and thus contribute to the emotional impact of the poem, their repetitive nature makes them efficient rhetorical devices which can "drive home" the message, thus contributing to the impact of the poem on the mind. The musical qualities of poetic form are often used for semantic purposes: strong metrical positions can emphasise the key words, and end rhymes stand out much more prominently than simple line breaks. Rhyme is also capable of linking together words that would not otherwise be linked, to create additional shades of meaning: see, for example, note 8 on p. 45.

Furthermore, established poetic forms have cultural significance rooted in the poetic canon. Importantly for translation, many Russian forms were initially borrowed, along with their intentions, associations and expectations, from the European poetic tradition. Consequently, there is no real need for complex (and seldom successful) inter-cultural mapping.

Poetic form supports a range of special effects. In "A drunk – less often, less willing..." by Yan Satunovsky (p. 106) the gradual descent from fully rhymed syllabic-accentual verse through partially rhymed accentual verse to *vers libre* emphasises the change of tone from self-deprecating and confessional through philosophical to dark and bitter. It would hardly be possible to achieve this by words alone in such a short poem. Similarly, Olzhas Suleimenov used form to make his poem "Every night someone steadily rides through my dream..." (p. 222) feel at once unmistakably Oriental (interlocking rubaiyat, equally exotic in Russian and English), very Russian (a disguised 8-liner in a ternary metre) and nearly Italian (the tight *aaba bbab* rhyme scheme, which resembles the beginning of a sonnet, and which creates a similar level of intensity).[1]

Last but not least, the demands of form contribute to the balance between freedom of expression and certain structural constraints, which is essential for art. In the words of W. H. Auden,

Blessed be all metrical rules that forbid automatic responses,
Force us to have second thoughts, free from the fetters of Self.

The interplay between meaning and form is one of the corner-stones of the Russian poetic tradition:

> Rhyme, rhythm, meter, and stanza have defined poetry for cen-turies, and in Russia (where free verse has never achieved more than marginal status) they continue to define poetry today. Any attempt to determine "what the poem means" must necessarily consider how the poet chooses to express this meaning. Questions of verse technique, in short, are not tangential to a poet's concerns. (Wachtel 1998: 2)

Consequently, the integrity of a poem inevitably suffers when its form is not adequately conveyed in translation: as Yevgeny Yevtushenko once put it, "Но если музыку погубишь, / Все мысли это переврет" (But if you let the music perish, / The thoughts will also sound quite false).[2] Another Russian poet corroborates this:

> It should be remembered that verse meters in themselves are kinds of spiritual magnitudes for which nothing can be substituted. They cannot be replaced even by each other, let alone by free verse. Differences in meters are differences in breath and in heart-beat. Differences in rhyming pattern are those of brain functions. (Brodsky 1986: 141)

The practice of ignoring the original form in literary translation into English is time-honoured. Introductions to some antholo-gies of translated Russian poetry give the impression that the transliteration system for the authors' names is a deeper and more interesting problem than the approach to translating their poems. In (Langland et al. 1973), (Weissbort 1974), (Reavey 1981), (McKane 1990), (Johnson and Ashby 1992) and (McKane 2003) abandoning the poetic form is assumed to be the natural order of things which does not even merit a discus-sion.[3] Olga Carlisle describes the compromises involved in capturing the meaning in poetic translation (1970: xii–xiv) but does not say a word about the form. R. A. D. Ford states that "Russian is easier to translate into English, keeping the feel of the original, than into other European languages" (1987: 13), but his translations still dispense with the metre, rhyme scheme and, in some cases, even the stanzaic form of the originals, as those presumably were not deemed important for the feel of the poems. Glad and Weissbort described and justified their strategy with respect to form ("rhythmic but unrhymed verse") in the early version of their anthology (1978: lx), but dropped the Note on Translation from the 1992 edition.

When applied with skill and sensitivity, approaches such as these can yield works of merit, but the results are best described as English poems inspired by the Russian originals, rather than as proper translations. While this has the obvious advantage that the results look natural to readers of contemporary English poetry, the alternative (preserving or approximating the form) is the only way to enable an Anglophone reader to feel how poetry is experienced by a native speaker of Russian. In the words of Walter Arndt,

> The goal is to create a poem in the target language, which would simulate, as near as may be, the total effect produced by the original on the contemporary reader. Total effect to me means *import* as well as *impact*, i.e., both what the poem imparts to the mind and how it strikes the senses; cognitive as well as aesthetic (stylistic, formal, musical, "poetic") values, pretending for just a moment that these two congruent entities can somehow be analytically separated. Again, "import as well as impact" means import *through* and *congruent with* impact; it does not mean a message in garbled prose, with subsequent assurances by way of stylistic and other commentary that the corpse in its lifetime was poetry. (1972: xlv–xlvi)

One common objection is that some readers might find effective formal translations very unconventional; Peter Levi, for example, counts adherence to metre amongst "the most rebarbative aspects of Russian verse to English readers" (McKane 1990: ix). However, this is not necessarily a bad thing: 20th-century Russian poetry is genuinely different from today's English poetry in its undiminished formal needs.

> "O.K.", a young American poet or reader of poetry may conclude after perusing [modern English translations from Mandelstam], "the same thing goes on over there in Russia." But what goes on over there is not at all the same thing. Apart from her metaphors, Russian poetry has set an example of moral purity and firmness, which to no small degree has been reflected in the preservation of the so-called classical forms without any damage to content. Herein lies her distinction from her Western sisters, though in no way

does one presume to judge whom this distinction favors most. However, it is a distinction, and if only for purely ethnographic reasons, that quality ought to be preserved in translation and not forced into some common mold. (Brodsky 1986: 142–143)

Owing to this difference, a translation preserving the form of the original should be permitted to sound somewhat unusual. Willis Barnstone argues in 'An ABC of Translating Poetry':

> Fray Luis de León wrote that translated poems should not appear foreign but as "nacidas en él y naturales" (as if born and natural in the language). Yet why not some flagrant unnaturalness? Why not shake up English poetry with the sudden arrogant figure of Vladimir Mayakovsky, standing tall in his coalminer's cap, shouting his syllables out to the sky from the Brooklyn Bridge? …

> Lexical shock renews weary language bones. It is good to drink Turkish coffee in the pampas of the American Midwest. (1993: 266)

This does not mean that all Russian forms are bound to sound alien in English. "Not a somnambulist's, my sleep is with my feet..." by Ivan Zhdanov (p. 294) is written in blank iambic pentameter and ends with a Shakespearean reference, which confirms that the form was chosen for a reason. It is difficult to see in what ways the linear prose translation "Not a sleep-walker, I sleep with my feet..." found in (High 2000: 128) sounds more natural than our congruent translation: iambic pentameter is known to match the cadence of English speech particularly well, and it tends to impart a certain gravity, which is very appropriate for this poem.

Another popular objection to preserving the form is based on a potential false association:

> In English-language verse, "formalism" is a rallying cry for a movement. In Russian, it is nothing of the kind; innovation and experimentation in poetry do not necessarily challenge traditional forms … To render all of these poets in an exact formal equivalent would seem to ally them with an English-language movement they do not necessarily adhere to. (Bunimovich and Kates 2007: xvii–xviii)

A variation of the same objection is the view that the presence of metre and rhyme automatically gives the translation an archaic feel, which may misrepresent the character of the original. A good way of addressing arguments of this type would be to imagine the same approach taken in an anthology of modern English poetry translated into Russian. An introductory note might read: "In Russian-language verse, *vers libre* is a rallying cry for a movement. In English, it is nothing of the kind; free verse has long become the norm and does not necessarily indicate innovation or experimentation. To render all of these poets in free verse would seem to ally them with a Russian-language movement they do not necessarily adhere to." Yet nobody to date has rendered English *vers libre* into Russian in rhymed metrical verse. The additional effort would not be an issue for a Russian verse translator, especially given that an original of this sort does not suggest or prohibit any particular rhyme scheme or metrical form. Could it be that translators into Russian trust the reader to understand the differences between the two poetic traditions? Would it not be equally logical to do the same in verse translation into English?

Assuming that the translator aims to preserve the poetic form, what exactly should be captured? It is immediately evident from even a superficial look at the Russian poetic canon that its defining formal feature is the presence of a metre, either syllabic-accentual or accentual. The organising role of metre in poetry is not unlike its role in music: the rhythmic structure, the basic drumbeat of the piece. Similar to the musical metre, the poetic one has a profound effect on the audience regardless of whether or not it is conceptualised:

> it is by *hearing* and repeating verse that the average Russian comes to recognize meters and – given sufficient time and interest – to associate certain ones with certain genres or themes. Such knowledge generally has no connection to nomenclature; one can recognize amphibrachs without knowing the traditional designation for them, just as one can sing a melody correctly without knowing musical notation. (Wachtel 1998: 259)

End rhyme comes second: there are many examples of unrhymed, metrical Russian poems, but rhymed verse with no metre is very rare in this language (while *vers libre* has its small niche in the canon). Continuing the analogy with music, the rhyme scheme is the tonality of the piece, which can be mobile or occasionally absent altogether; while there can be no music (in the conventional sense) without metre.

Other formal features, such as alliterations or internal rhymes, are often present in Russian poetry, but they fall short of having the defining status: it is generally the metre and the end rhymes that make a Russian poem formally complete, and this was as true in the 20th century as it was in earlier periods.[4] It is impossible to convey the Russian poetic form (and therefore the full meaning of a Russian poem) in translation without retaining its metrical properties and rhyme scheme, where present.

Matching the Russian Form in English

There are no fundamental obstacles to preserving metre and rhyme when translating from Russian into English. Both languages are stress-timed and the mainstream types of formal verse in both languages are syllabic-accentual and accentual, each type based on the same basic mechanisms in English and in Russian. The concept of rhyme also manifests itself in similar ways in these languages, albeit with considerable quantitative differences which reflect their differing morphologies. Using George Szirtes's metaphor of formal poetry as a dance with the language (2006), one could say that the English language is quite capable of dancing to Russian music, and can do so with flair and dignity, even though it may not be the most natural of dances for it.

There are, however, important differences between the Russian and English prosodic systems, which have a bearing on our way of reproducing the Russian form in English translation. The rest of this section looks at the techniques for exploiting the similarities and overcoming the differences.

Readers lacking basic understanding of prosody may wish to skip to the next section (p. xxxviii) or refer to an introductory publication on these matters, such as (Fry 2005) or (Steele 1999). A thorough analysis of the formal features of Russian verse, done from the English perspective but without translation in mind, can be found in (Scherr 1986).

Metre

Both Russian and English prosodies distinguish between syllabic-accentual verse, with its accurately timed, steady pulse based on the count of syllables and on the exact positions of word stresses, and accentual verse, whose rhythmic propulsion comes from the natural phrasal stresses of freely flowing speech, occasionally helped along by alliteration or lesser sonorities. The distinction is more subtle in English, where "word stress" is as much syntagmatic as it is lexical, but the difference between the two systems is still clear in this language and can be directly reflected in translation.

Russian prosody has an additional verse form called *dolnik*, which is a compromise between accentual and syllabic-accentual paradigms. It allows for either one or two unstressed syllables between word stresses, and is excellent for maintaining the listener's interest through continual rhythmic variation. *Dolnik* was introduced by early modernists in their translations from European languages, and was adopted by many poets in the beginning of the 20th century (Alexander Blok being a prime exponent: see p. 12). It gradually lost its popularity, but was brought back, in modified form with a strong logaoedic tendency, by Joseph Brodsky (an example can be found on p. 268). *Dolnik* can be rendered in English as accentual verse of the same number of beats, but only allowing one or two off-beat syllables between them. This gives the resulting "English *dolnik*" a Russian character, especially if the reader is familiar with the original concept.[5]

In both languages the foreground rhythm of syllabic-accentual verse, represented by the lexical and phrasal stresses, is not enslaved by the background metrical beat; rather, the two form a loose hierarchy where the background is compulsive but permissive of some contradiction. The weaker English stress, which leads to a higher tolerance of foot inversions, creates additional opportunities in that respect: the occasional freedom enjoyed by the poetic foreground in this language is not dissimilar to what a jazz player experiences when he runs ahead of the bass rhythm, only to slip slightly behind it before finally culminating in a perfectly timed cadence. By contrast, Russian verse reserves its very conspicuous foot inversions and hypermetrical stresses for special effects; the polyphony of metre and rhythm manifests itself in this language mainly via unrealised stresses in binary feet (called "scuds" in Nabokov 1964) – a phenomenon which is known in English prosody as the pyrrhic substitution. This difference has an underlying linguistic reason: Russian words are mostly polysyllabic, as befits a synthetic language, and can only have one stress; in the relatively analytic English language words are much shorter on average, and usually possess a secondary stress when they happen to be long. Consequently, maintaining an actual lexical stress on every second syllable in a sufficiently long line of Russian iamb or trochee would be impossible without severely restricting the vocabulary (which was, in fact, tried and quickly abandoned by the 18th-century pioneers of Russian syllabic-accentual versification). This is why an unrealised stress does not violate the metre in Russian verse; only a stress in the wrong place does. In practical terms this means that, on the one hand, a translator from Russian into English gets a very welcome additional freedom in the target language (occasional foot inversions); on the other hand, capturing the characteristic music of Russian syllabic-accentual verse demands a higher emphasis on pyrrhic substitutions and fewer occurrences of foot inversions than one tends to observe in English poetry of this type.

The differences in the average length of words and in the strength and metrical treatment of accentuation also have implications for the prevailing metrical schemes in the languages in question. Amphibrach (∪–∪ ∪–∪ ...) is nearly unheard of in English poetry, because adding or dropping a single unstressed syllable in the beginning of a line turns this symmetrical metre into either anapaest (∪∪– ∪∪– ...) or dactyl (–∪∪ –∪∪ ...), either of which satisfies the English preference for rising or falling metres. Some classifications do not even include amphibrach in the system of English metres, treating it as dactyl with an anacrusis. In Russian prosody amphibrach is an ordinary metre, which is not easily confused with dactyl or anapaest and which, together with its ternary siblings, is a good match for the average ratio of one stress per 2¾ syllables characteristic of the Russian language. Amphibrach is also quite popular with poets. Rendering it in English involves a battle against the strong tendency of the language to slip into dactyl or anapaest. It is questionable to what extent this battle can be won, but the metre should at least be given a fair chance. The difference in sound and established functions between binary and ternary metres in Russian poetry is much stronger than the differences between amphibrach and its siblings, so the negative effects of confusing amphibrach with dactyl or anapaest in translation are small.

Quaternary metres are also affected by the matters of word length and stress. Paeons are seldom seen in Russian poetry because the native listener's ear is so used to sliding over the inevitable missing stresses that a paeonic foot is likely to be perceived as two binary feet, one of them pyrrhic ($\cup\cup$), unless the poet manages to establish a very stable pattern right in the beginning of the piece, as Innokenty Annensky does in his poem on p. 6. This feature of the Russian paeons allows a translator to render them in English in a binary metre without significant violation of the form.

Imitations of classical metres (i.e. epic hexameter and elegiac distich) present an interesting case. They seldom occur in Russian poetry other than in translations from Greek or Latin, and in the 20th century they were used almost exclusively to create a clear reference to a classical framework, often for the comical or ironic effect caused by the resultant clash with modern realities. To preserve this artistically important quality in translation it would be logical to use a conventional way of imitating the corresponding classical metre in English. This is done in slightly different ways in the two prosodic systems. For example, the six-beat accentual metre can be successfully deployed in English to imitate epic hexameter, but in Russian this metre does not produce the required effect, and a relaxed dactylic hexameter (which allows for the dropping one, or even both, unstressed syllables in certain feet) is used instead. With this in mind, reproducing the exact metrical structure of a mock classical Russian original, as we do on p. 241, may be a reasonable approach in some cases, but it cannot be the goal: the form of the translation should hark back directly to the classical prototype rather than its Russian imitation.

Caesura plays a prominent role in Russian verse. Its rhythmic strength can vary widely: from an essential pause similar to that of Old English alliterative verse (p. 252) to merely a word boundary at the same metrical point in every line (p. 268). Caesura does not exist as a formal feature in modern English versification, so we render the Russian caesura by enforcing a word boundary regardless of its intended strength. The goal is to make sure that the intonation created by the caesura in the original can be reproduced when reciting the translation without splitting or stretching English words.

Neither English nor Russian limits the range of stress positions within a word, so the difference between masculine ($'$), feminine ($' \cup$), dactylic ($' \cup\cup$) and other endings, which plays an important role in Russian verse,[6] can be reproduced in English directly. However, from the English perspective the difference in intonation between feminine and longer endings is small compared to the difference between masculine endings and endings of any other kind, especially when rhyme is involved. Some classifications even take the view that there are only two kinds of endings in English verse: masculine and feminine. This is an important consideration for a translator.

Rhyme

It is true that the exuberance of rhyme in Russian is not matched by the English language. Henry Hewlett's essay (1891) contains an excellent analysis of the nature, extent and implications of this difficulty, albeit his comparison is between English and the Romance languages. This linguistic characteristic is often cited as the reason for the predominance of unrhymed translations into English, but it is only a quantitative issue.[7]

The contrast between the rhyming powers of the English and Russian languages decreased in the 20th century, which saw movement towards lesser, assonant and consonant, rhymes in Russian poetry. Few would argue that English is anything less than capable of producing such rhymes; moreover, in many cases a mere semblance of rhyme is all that is needed to represent the all-important sound patterns of the original.[8] When such rhymes are permitted in translation, the degrees of "natural rhymability" of the languages in question do not appear to be very different. In this volume we take this approach for modern and traditional rhymes alike, which is unavoidable: as Glad and Weissbort rightly pointed out (1978: lx), the equivalent of a Russian rhyme is not necessarily a rhyme of equal strength in English.

Feminine ($' \cup$) and dactylic ($' \cup\cup$) rhymes are widely used in Russian poetry; rendering them in a language where much of the common vocabulary is monosyllabic is a serious challenge.

There are a limited number of avenues to explore within the confines of conventional English prosody:

- Nontrivially rhyming longer words, such as "beckoned"-"second" (Pushkin and Arndt, 1981: 150) or "weather"-"together" (Pushkin and Johnston 1979: 44). Rhymes of this type are relatively hard to come by in English, and it is important not to get overly creative with them lest the text should feel contrived. There is also the risk of repetitiveness: for example in (Pushkin and Falen 1998: 5) the rhyme "brother"-"other" re-appears in the second stanza of the work, having already been spent in the form of "others"-"brothers" in the first stanza.
- Homoeoteleuton rhymes: "badly"-"sadly", "admonished"-"astonished", "falling"-"recalling", "waking"-"breaking", "breathing"-"wreathing", etc. The examples are taken from *Onegin*-inspired *The Golden Gate* (Seth 1986); the latter three, incredibly, appear in the same stanza, 6.1. Excessive reliance on such rhymes can make verse predictable and boring.
- Mosaic rhymes, e.g. "splendour"-"send her" (Pushkin and Johnston 1979: 43). Their use in English poetry goes back at least as far as Byron: in the Dedication to his *Don Juan*, "posterity" is rhymed with "to spare it, he". This type of rhyme became more common in the 20th century; it seems logical to use it when translating Russian poetry of that period into English.

In practice, the translator has to utilise all these techniques, mixing them in the right proportion according to the nature of the original rhymes and the overall style of the author (whether classical or modern). However, this arsenal is not quite sufficient when dealing with originals where half of the rhymes are feminine, which is typical of Russian poetry.

An additional degree of freedom is provided by flexible treatment of diphthongs in rhymes. While technically forming a masculine ending in the final syllable of a line, English diphthongs often sound as one and a half vowels in such positions. The Russian language has no true diphthongs of its own, and from the Russian perspective the intonation of English diphthongs at a line end is somewhere in between the intonations of masculine and feminine endings. We utilise this perception by treating diphthongs in the final syllable as capable of participating in both masculine ("throb"-"globe", p. 113) and feminine ("flying"-"clown", p. 249) rhymes. As an extension of this approach, pairs of diphthong endings ("glare"-"dare", p. 221) can be allowed to represent the feminine rhymes of the Russian originals. Walter Arndt uses this technique in his classical translation of *Eugene Onegin*, albeit very occasionally: e.g. "coach"-"approach" (Pushkin and Arndt 1981: 39). Our position is that allowing the feminine interpretation of diphthongal rhymes is a natural way of reflecting the length of Russian clausula in translation while still respecting the strong predilection for masculine rhymes in English. When reciting such lines, a fuller enunciation of the final diphthong is advisable where the form of the piece suggests a feminine rhyme.

Finally, as has already been mentioned in the discussion of the difference in intonation between different kinds of endings on p. xxix, systematic rendering of dactylic or hyperdactylic Russian rhymes as feminine or diphthongal could be an acceptable compromise in some cases (see p. 249).

> There is a tendency among English and American translators of Russian poetry ... to replace feminine rhymes with the masculine rhymes with which most English readers feel more comfortable. This tendency should, I think, be resisted. However, the parallel tendency to replace dactylic rhymes by feminine ones ... is more acceptable, given the difficulty of making dactylic rhymes work in serious English poetry. (Kline 1994: 48)

Other formal features

Alliterations and occasional internal rhymes often have to be sacrificed in order to reproduce the key meaning and the primary form of the original. One degree of freedom available for rendering artistically important alliterations is the choice of the repeated sound: the translator has to establish whether that sound refers to, or hints at, something specific or is repeated for purely melodic purposes achieved by the repetition as such. Accordingly, the translation may need to produce a closely matching sound, a sound of a specific kind (such as the hissing *s*, associated with the annoyed cat and matching the growling Russian *r* of the original, found in the last stanza on p. 235), or any repeated sound. Vowel for vowel and consonant for consonant is usually a safe bet when attempting to reproduce non-specific Russian alliterations in English: see, for example,

p. 93, where "на сне́жную **ширь** / Вышел кружи́ть" is rendered as "that's **flown** / **Ov**er **w**ide sn**ow**fields".

The deliberate repetition of a word or an expression, usually at the beginning of several lines (anaphora), may be an important feature of the original. However, it is not always possible to achieve a similar placement of the corresponding English words because of the syntactic differences between the two languages. In order to find the best way of rendering an anaphora, it is necessary to assess its artistic function in the original and to establish whether the repetition is semantically or syntactically driven. In some cases the solution may involve a different kind of repetition or no repetition at all. For example, the first six lines of the poem on p. 96 all start with the same conjunctive, but such a construct (a list with "and" in front of each item including the first) is awkward in English. The translation attempts to approximate the "piling on" effect through the intensifying combination of "time and again", "all those" and "make me recall" in the final line of the poem, where the original in fact eases off and reads merely "remind me of you every time".

Enjambment effectively plays the same role in Russian and English verse, except that is has to be very prominent or systematic in Russian to be artistically significant. Despite the inevitable interference with end rhymes, it is often possible to capture important enjambments. The last stanza on p. 309 gives an example of a very deliberate chain of enjambments that has been reproduced in the translation, breaking the line in between the same words as in the original virtually every time, while preserving the rhymes.

Word order

Russian versification takes full advantage of the inflectional nature of the language: the syntactic functions of the words are, in many cases, held in place by morphology regardless of the word order. The predicate may follow the subject and precede the object, but it can just as well assume the first or last position in the sentence. This freedom is utilised in poetry in several ways:

- Different orders highlight different parts of the sentence, which helps to accentuate the intended focus.

- Depending on the chosen word order different parts of speech may occur in a rhyming position, which helps to avoid the monotony of homoeoteleuton rhymes.
- Choosing a suitable word order is a common way of satisfying metrical constraints.

The English language has the standard subject-verb-object (SVO) order, which is semantically strict. Nevertheless, English poetry has seen numerous occasions of word order violation, of the kind that philologists refer to as anastrophe. The best known of these are probably Emily Dickinson's poems, where examples such as this abound:

> Till ranks of seeds their witness bear –
> And softly thro' the altered air
> Hurries a timid leaf.

Here we have two inverted clauses coordinated by a conjunct: one is an SOV, the other a more drastic VS which can still easily be parsed thanks to the unambiguously adverbial phrase "through the altered air".

Twentieth-century English poets may have been less liberal than Emily Dickinson, but their use of anastrophe is common enough not to be treated as an oddity. Noun-adjective inversions, such as "pastures new", are so common that they should probably be treated as being within the general syntax of the poetic language. Furthermore, some poets (for instance, John Betjeman) make frequent use of the SOV structure, in particular for placing a verb in the rhyming position:

> And London shops on Christmas Eve
> Are strung with silver bells and flowers
> As hurrying clerks the City leave
> to pigeon-haunted classic towers.

Here the anastrophe helps to maintain the iambic tetrameter, provides a perfect rhyme ("Eve"-"leave") and gives the line a subliminal emphasis: the clerks *leave* their place of work, wherever it is, on Christmas Eve.

The incidence of anastrophe varies a great deal among 20th-century poets. Philip Larkin, for example, does not use it often at all. Despite this, a rather daring example can be found in his poetry:

> I'll show you, come to that,
> the bracken where I never trembling sat.

Even Ezra Pound, a well-known proponent of natural expression in poetry, allowed himself the following VS structure:

> Then sat we amidships, wind jamming the tiller.

It is hard to argue, therefore, that in translating Russian poetry the standard English word order should be adhered to at all costs. After all, the translator is already disadvantaged by the lesser availability and poorer quality of rhymes in English. When this is further aggravated by the need to achieve a certain focus, the compromise in the word order should be put on the table alongside the compromises in other areas: rhyming quality, the fullness of rendering the original semantics, etc. It is, of course, quite necessary to make sure that the use of anastrophe is as smooth and infrequent as possible. The translator should also be aware of how much penalty is associated with its various structures. Based on our observations of established 20th-century poetic practice and, to some extent, on the translator's personal taste, we have come up with the following guidelines:

- The post-positioning of adjectives can be used liberally, provided that it does not create a spurious pattern.
- The SOV structure presents little difficulty in parsing and should be assumed to impose only a small penalty.
- The OSV structure feels more natural, but it is also prone to confusion as the reader may misinterpret some objects as subjects in the absence of clear lexical markers.
- OVS (often called locative inversion) has some idiomatic use, but otherwise can only be acceptable in special cases, as it does feel quite contrived.

The use of anastrophe is not uniform in the Anthology. 'Kulikovo' by D. A. Prigov (pp. 274–276) is one example that verges on the avant-garde in the original. A long string of skilfully shaded near-identical verbal rhymes in the first stanza, where varying prefixes (nine in total) are responsible for a seemingly infinite variation of meaning, contributes to the comical effect and creates a surprise without which the poem would lose its lustre. It was imperative for us to retain this feature, and so all means – including borderline anastrophe – were employed.

The freedom of the order of words in Russian sentences is not unlimited, so it is possible for the originals to contain syntactic inversions of their own. Using the OVS word order is one way of rendering an artistically important anastrophe, but as there is no parallelism between the Russian and English grammars in this matter, it is often appropriate to re-create the intended effect by entirely different means.

The mapping table

The following table summarises our approach to rendering Russian poetic form in English:

Russian	English
The number of lines and the stanzaic form	Reproduced exactly.
The length of syllabic-accentual metre	Matched exactly if stable. Matched approximately if it varies.
Trochee $-\cup$	Trochee. Pyrrhic ($\cup\cup$) substitutions preferred to iambic. No iambic substitutions for old-fashioned originals.
Iamb $\cup-$	Iamb. Pyrrhic substitutions preferred to trochaic. No trochaic substitutions for old-fashioned originals.
Dactyl $-\cup\cup$	Dactyl. No binary substitutions.
Amphibrach $\cup-\cup$	Amphibrach. Special care to be taken not to provoke dactylic or anapaestic reading. No binary substitutions.
Anapaest $\cup\cup-$	Anapaest. No binary substitutions.

Russian	English
Paeons $-\cup\cup\cup$ *(1st)* $\cup-\cup\cup$ *(2nd)* $\cup\cup-\cup$ *(3rd)* $\cup\cup\cup-$ *(4th)*	The corresponding paeon for originals with a very obvious quaternary metre. Trochee (for the first and third paeons) or iamb (for the second and fourth paeons) of twice the length can be substituted otherwise, following the mapping system for binary metres.
Logaoedic metres	The same feet in the same order.
Dolnik	Accentual verse with the same number of beats and 1–2 unstressed syllables between the stresses: "English *dolnik*".
Imitative classical metres	The same classical metre imitated according to the English prosodic conventions.
Caesura	Word boundary observed at the same metrical point if the original has a stable pattern. May be ignored otherwise.
Accentual verse	Accentual verse with the same number of beats. Approximate match of the syllable count. No need to match the positions of stresses.
Idiosyncratic metrical arrangements	Dealt with individually, in keeping with the overall nature of the original. The same general principles as for the primary metres.

Russian	English
Masculine, feminine or long endings and rhymes	Reproduced if the original has an identifiable pattern of ending types.
	Diphthongs in the final syllable may be used to render feminine endings.
	Diphthongs in the penultimate syllable may account for two metrical positions when rendering dactylic rhymes.
	Dactylic and hyperdactylic rhymes may be systematically represented by feminine rhymes as a compromise.
Rhyme scheme	The same scheme for originals with a clear pattern.
	A similar scheme for less regular patterns.
Quality of rhyme	Matched in obviously special cases, such as identical rhyme.
	Assonant and consonant rhymes allowed elsewhere.
	Mosaic rhymes deployed when necessary.
Alliterations and other sonorities	Matched by similar effects when very prominent in the original or essential for its design.
	May be ignored otherwise.
	The actual repeated sound may be different unless there is a clear reason to keep the sound of the original.
Anaphora	Matched by a similar repetition if syntactically possible.
	Other means of achieving the required effect deployed if necessary.

Russian	English
Enjambment	Reproduced when there is a clear artistic function involved or when there is a system behind its use: the design of the original, the individual style of the poet etc.
Anastrophe	Only very prominent syntactical inversions found in the original need to be reproduced (or rendered by other means).
	Inversion may be introduced to create a focus or to maintain the metre or rhyme scheme. SOV and OSV orders are strongly preferred to OVS in such cases.
	Caution to be taken to avoid syntactical confusion.

Congruent Translation: Trying Harder

The word "congruent" in the book title refers to a specific kind of correspondence: one which is based on our understanding of the defining features of Russian poetic form and the differences between Russian and English versification outlined in the previous section. Our guiding principle has been strict metrical observance with a liberal but persistent use of rhyme, with the specific requirements for the primary Russian metres and commonly occurring formal features listed in the mapping table above.

One way to describe what we are aiming to achieve could be through the following rather extreme validation procedure: we consider a translation congruent if its formally complete units (usually stanzas) can be interleaved with those of the original to produce a viable chimera – that is, an artefact which would be accepted by bilingual readers as a valid, if unusual, version of the original poem. As an illustration, here are two such chimeras derived from a poem by Osip Mandelstam and its congruent translation:

LENINGRAD

Я вернулся в мой город, знакомый до слёз,
До прожилок, до детских припухлых желёз.

You've returned to this place, take a gulp here at once
Of the cod oil of Leningrad's riverside lamps.

Узнавай же скорее декабрьский денек,
Где к зловещему дегтю подмешан желток.

Petersburg, I am not ready yet to be dead:
You've my telephone numbers, the record is set.

Петербург! У меня еще есть адреса,
По которым найду мертвецов голоса.

My stairwell is a dark one. My temple is hit
When the torn-out door bell starts to peal in a fit.

И всю ночь напролет жду гостей дорогих,
Шевеля кандалами цепочек дверных.

•

ЛЕНИНГРАД

I've returned to the city I know really well:
By the tears and the veinlets, by mumps' painful swell.

Ты вернулся сюда, так глотай же скорей
Рыбий жир ленинградских речных фонарей,

Recognise the December daylight at a stroke,
Where the ominous tar is mixed up with a yolk.

Петербург! я еще не хочу умирать!
У тебя телефонов моих номера.

Furthermore, I have many a private address,
Where the voice I could find of a person erased.

Я на лестнице черной живу, и в висок
Ударяет мне вырванный с мясом звонок,

And awaiting dear guests, I'm awake every night,
With the door's swinging manacles fixed in my sight.

One could also think of a weaker procedure, which does not
require the validator's knowledge of Russian: to read the
translation in sync with the original, which is slowly read aloud
by someone else.

To say that congruent Russian-English translation of poetry is possible in principle is not to say that it is an easy thing to do, which at least partially explains why translations of this kind are so few and far between. However, they do exist. *Eugene Onegin* can be read in a number of congruent translations, e.g. (Pushkin and Arndt 1981), (Pushkin and Falen 1998), (Pushkin and Hofstadter 2000), (Pushkin and Johnston 1979) or (Pushkin and Mitchell 2008).[9] The works of 19th-century poets selected for (Brodsky and Myers 1988) have also been translated this way. Anatoly Liberman published collections of congruent translations from Lermontov (1984) and Tyutchev (1993). As far as the 20th century is concerned, here are some examples of translations that follow principles similar to ours:

- 'Loneliness' by Ivan Bunin, translated by Yakov Hornstein (Yevtushenko et al. 1993: 23–24).
- "In everything I seek to grasp..." by Boris Pasternak, translated by Avril Pyman (Kupriyanova and Ivanovskaya 1981: 119–120).
- 'The Ivanovs' by Nikolai Zabolotsky, translated by Merrill Sparks (Markov and Sparks 1966: 685–689).
- 'Ah Nadya, Nadyenka' by Bulat Okudzhava, translated by Mark Herman and Ronnie Apter (Kates 1999: 25).
- Approximately half of the translations included in the bilingual edition of nativity poems by Joseph Brodsky (2001b), in particular 'January 1, 1965', translated by the author (ibid. 9) and "A second Christmas by the shore...", translated by George L. Kline (ibid. 49). Brodsky insisted on congruence; an interesting analysis of his position and of the strengths and weaknesses of the resulting "formally mimetic" translations can be found in Daniel Weissbort's review (2002) of *Collected Poems in English* (Brodsky 2001a).[10]

The arguments about the merits of preserving metre and rhyme often shy away from discussing, or even mentioning, the difficulties involved in it, as if they had nothing to do with the issue. One can therefore only admire the forthrightness with which Andrew Wachtel tackles it in his introductory article to a bilingual web anthology of Russian verse:

> We have elected, in the vast majority of cases, to preserve the meter of the eighteenth- and nineteenth-century selections, whereas the twentieth-century poems are generally rendered in free verse. We have opted not to rhyme the poems (although to this day most

Russian poetry is metered and rhymed), because to do so would force us to abandon all hope of staying close enough to the original to allow its idiosyncrasies to come through in translation. (Kutik and Wachtel 2006)

Willis Barnstone tells, by way of acknowledgement, an instructive story in his book on literary translation:

> Jorge Luis Borges, with whom I was working on the translation of his sonnets, conveyed through Carlos Frías that I had not found a good rhyme to go with "Walt Whitman", the last two words of a poem. I protested, and then Frías said diplomatically but firmly: "Borges says to try harder." Those words have sustained me for many years and have made things easier. (1993: ix)

This is echoed by J. Kates in the afterword to the bilingual anthology compiled and edited by him, and to which he also contributed his own translations:

> Once in Moscow I was reading my own poems – all of which begin in strict rhyme and meter, and many of which stay that way – as well as my translations of Mikhail Aizenberg. In the critical discussion that always follows a Russian poetry reading, I explained my reasons for translating the strict forms of the Russian verses into slightly looser structures in English – a practice understood and approved by Aizenberg. But one prominent critic stood up and commented, "That's all very well. You make a good case. But you should try harder."
>
> Since then, I have always tried harder. (1999: 417)

The Strategy

Our fundamental assumption is that aiming to preserve both the key image-making semantics and the essential poetic form does not create an irresolvable conflict. Indeed, there is usually enough non-key meaning in a poem to exploit: otherwise a poetic form could only be created by chance.

Many translators would disagree with this view and oppose any changes to the meaning of the original. Vladimir Nabokov is their vociferous champion:

> A tortured author and a deceived reader, this is the inevitable outcome of arty paraphrase. The only object and justification of translation is the conveying of the most exact information possible and

this can be only achieved by a literal translation, with notes. (Appel and Nabokov 1967: 143) [11]

Our view is that this position has two fundamental weaknesses:

- It must be based on the questionable assumption that all words of the original are equally important semantically.
- It ignores the fact that writing (not translating) rhymed metrical verse involves a compromise between potentially conflicting demands of meaning and form.

Poets writing in metre and rhyme admit that they occasionally struggle to find a word or an expression that would satisfy their chosen form. They even make humorous references to this in their works, for example in 'A Letter to General Z.' by Joseph Brodsky: "Генерал! Я взял вас для рифмы к слову / «умирал»" ("General, ... I'm using you, or, rather what you are, / to rhyme with 'funeral'" – Brodsky and Maxwell 2004). Taking such liberties can only be possible in segments of secondary importance: otherwise the result would be rhymed gibberish. Pushkin's manuscripts are full of incomplete lines where he evidently wrote down what he felt was important, which sometimes was the rhyme rather than anything else. The poet would eventually fill in the gaps, but what exactly should the translation produce in the target language? Ought it to be "the most exact information possible" contained in the gap-filling segments of the original text, or should it be an adequate rendition of the poetic form, for the sake of which the gaps were skilfully filled in the first place? Why should the translator not have the same freedom to alter words or expressions whose precise meaning is secondary to the poem in order to attain the same goal: to meet the demands of the form without adversely affecting the key meaning?

In short, we suggest reconciling the meaning and the form all over again on behalf of the author. In our view, this is the only way to preserve what Boris Pasternak famously called "точность тайн" (the precision of mysteries), compared with which the precision of meaning does not stand for much. The exact words chosen in the original are of course important, but they are secondary in importance to the two masters served by them: the image and the form.

> When Horace is translated word for word by students in a third-year Latin class, there is no artistic danger as long as it is understood that such methods are solely a testing device of a student's

mastery of Latin, and not to be confused with literary transfer. Cribs or glosses have no autonomy. They are never to be read alone but only as means of learning how to read the source language. (Barnstone 1993: 35)

It is surprising to what extent these fundamentally different tasks – the provision of a gloss and literary translation – can be confused. The bilingual anthology of contemporary Russian poetry compiled and translated by Gerald S. Smith expressly describes the translations as "mainly intended to provide a way into the original texts for Anglophone students of Russian poetry whose grasp of the language is not secure enough for them to proceed with these texts on their own" (1993: xxxv). This did not prevent a reviewer from making the following statement:

Smith provides serviceable translations of each poem, claiming neither elegance nor literary merit for his efforts. Most translations, however, do manage the balancing act of retaining some linguistic features of the original while adequately conveying the poet's general intent. (Peterson 1995: 235)

One is left wondering what kind of "general intent" on the part of a poet could be adequately conveyed without elegance or literary merit...

Our aim has been to produce autonomous works which could be read alone, and our approach should be deemed just as fair to the translation as it is to the original: the translator takes just as much liberty with the meaning for reproducing the form as the poet took to create it in the first place. Because of that, the results certainly qualify as translations rather than imitations in the Lowellian sense – "reckless with literal meaning". While Nabokov swears by "literal translation, with notes" (which are supposed to explain, amongst other things, the vanished poetic form of the original), we are proposing congruent translation, with notes explaining any significant changes to non-key meaning that have been tolerated for the sake of congruence.

From this point of view the modern approach to translating Russian poetry, which can be described in Nabokov's terms as "literal translation, without notes", is counterproductive: by slavishly translating the scaffolding elements while failing to reproduce the form that they were meant to support, such translations do the originals a double injustice. Paradoxically, the same fallacy often makes the resulting translations look more convincing: the scaffolding protruding into the air gives the text a certain mysterious quality, helping a willing reader to see the unmotivated idiosyncratic prose as highly artistic free verse and thus completing the illusion of poetry. Genuine *vers libre* translations cannot possibly be literal because of the requirement "to compose in the sequence of a musical phrase", as Ezra Pound put it.

The Method

Based on the reasoning outlined in the previous section, our method has been to separate the key image-making semantics of the original from what appears to have been chosen chiefly for the sake of form. The former needs to be conveyed literally or "sense for sense"; the latter may, without loss of poetic power, be rendered by similarly intended, rather than necessarily equivalent, words or phrases in the target language. An example of this is the use of the word "ellipse" instead of "oval" in our translation of Naum Korzhavin's poem on p. 157. The word овал is repeated four times in the original (including the epigraph), requiring a rhyme every time. The corresponding English word "oval" cannot be used in the respective positions because all those rhymes are masculine, a feature that should be preserved to maintain congruence. Substituting "ellipse" solves the technical problem and has no adverse effect on the meaning of the poem.

In rare cases, evidently "scaffolding" elements can even be translated as something entirely different semantically, but which creates a similar effect, provided that the translator is certain that the effect was what the original material was all about. For example, the words "правила деленья" (the rules of division) on p. 196 are not entirely logical (it is hard to imagine a university professor, rather than a junior-school teacher, needing the rules of division) and must have been chosen to create a wonderfully extended assonant rhyme with "смотрит на деревья" (is looking at the trees), which also sounded very modern in the 1950s Russia. Replacing the professor by a teacher of Latin in translation made it possible to reproduce the metre, the rhyme scheme and the hypnotic rhythm of the original, which are endlessly more important to the poem in question than the exact meaning of those "rules of division".

An even more daring substitution was undertaken when translating 'Yet There's That Duet...' by David Samoilov (see pp. 141–143). In the original it is a duet for violin and viola, as stated in the title and in the last lines of stanzas 4, 8 and 10 (the last occurrence being in the last line of the poem). Replacing so prominent a phrase was not an easy decision, even though "flute and violin" has the required metrical properties, supports a wide choice of rhymes and is musically plausible for the composer in question. The most important factor in favour of the replacement was the understanding that the poem is not really about music, but art and artists in general, so the exact combination of instruments in the duet, or the fact that Mozart apparently never wrote a duet for flute and violin, is of little importance to its message.

Some substitutions are thrust upon the translator by the target language itself. In the original of 'The Harp on an Irish Coin' by Vladimir Krivulin on p. 280 пенье (singing) is rhymed with пенни (penny). Rhyming "singing" with "shilling" – a coin also embossed with a harp on the reverse – is obviously the way things were meant to be in English. There is a semantic bonus here as well: the shilling is a distinctive element of the pre-decimal £sd currency system, and thus the word provides a hint to the correct period for Anglophone readers (while perceptive Russian readers would recognise the early 1950s from other references in the original).

The difference between key and non-key meaning is, of course, not absolute: it is a matter of degree. Each word or phrase used in a poem has its semantic value, determined by analysis of the original, within the range that stretches from "absolutely key to the overall meaning" to "an essentially form-driven choice". Depending on its value, the word/phrase may either only allow a close or tolerate a liberal substitution to achieve congruence: rendering "oval" as "ellipse" is not the same thing as substituting a teacher for a professor, modifying the topic discussed by him and changing the overall setting from university to school. The congruence of a translation is equally a matter of degree: for example, our version of 'Six Years Since' by Joseph Brodsky (pp. 265–267) is more congruent than the translation 'Six Years Later' by Richard Wilbur (Brodsky 2001a: 3–4). Not only do we preserve the masculine and feminine endings, we also reproduce the exquisite self-similar structure where the special rhyme scheme (*aaBccB* rather than *aBaBcc*) of stanzas 3 and 6 mirrors, in the placement of the indented lines *B*, the placement of those two special stanzas within the original. This feature of the poem is an integral part of its overall design inspired by the number in the title – six stanzas of six lines each – and as such needs to be reflected in a form-preserving translation.

There is, however, one essential pre-requisite to applying our method: knowing what is part of the poem's scaffolding and what is not. This is inevitably a matter of discerning judgement; the translator's success depends to a large extent on the quality of this judgement, just as the beauty of the original verse depends on its author's keenness of ear and vision – besides, that is, a fine sense of form. A thorough understanding of the original is paramount: preserving a meaning only makes sense when it is understood correctly with all its contextual, cultural and literary subtleties; modifying it also requires a very clear idea of what one is deviating from. A good example of what may happen otherwise is given by the following fragment of a conversation between Seamus Heaney and Robert Hass at the Townsend Center for the Humanities, Berkeley:

> How much departure do you allow yourself? I don't know if this is a good example but it is an example of my moral issue around this – there is this poem in Pasternak's *My Sister Life* that contains an image of a summer storm. It contains a line that goes something like "Raindrops like collar studs blind the garden." And I read the versions of a friend of mine, and the last line said "raindrops – like cufflinks – blind the garden," and I said, ... "What the hell?" And he said, "Well I didn't think people would know what collar studs are." And I said, "That's too bad." I think that you don't want to change the image in that way. (2000: 19)

This is very interesting, but completely misguided. The word запонки in that poem by Pasternak is a generic term describing cufflinks, shirt studs or collar studs; it would normally be understood as cufflinks when used by itself. In fact, there is no dedicated word for collar studs in Russian; the usual way of referring to them is through that generic term: "запонки для воротника" (links/studs for a collar). The line in question reads "У капель — тяжесть запонок" (the raindrops are as heavy as cufflinks / shirt studs / collar studs). There is no way to know for sure which type of fastening Pasternak had in mind in this hyperbole, but the reference to weight makes cufflinks the most likely candidate as the heaviest of the three. Not that it matters: the language, and hence the culture, of the original makes no fundamental distinction between those items, so there can be no moral issue here, only a technical choice on the part of the translator.[12]

The overall degree of freedom afforded by the original to a congruent translator depends on various factors; the most obvious being the length of lines and metrical restrictions. Translating short rhymed lines in strict metre is very difficult, but so was writing them. Therefore some compromises must have been made by the original author, resulting in the presence of non-key meaning which can be adjusted to achieve congruence. Page 135 gives an example of congruent translation in the space of 2–4 syllables per rhymed metrical line: the original contains only three words (not counting prepositions and conjunctives) that do not rhyme with anything. Longer lines and a relaxed metre create room for manoeuvre and require fewer substitutions. An example of virtually no interference with the meaning for the sake of form can be found in the last stanza on p. 261, which deviates from the semantics of the original only in one minor respect: the action of оглянись (look back) is implied rather than rendered expressly. Strictly speaking, the translation also contains one word which has no direct counterpart in the original, but in fact "stone well" is used instead of "well" for a semantic reason, to disambiguate a water-well from a borehole (the Russian word колодец means unambiguously the former); the translator did, of course, establish that Abraham's Well was stone-enclosed. Everything else in that stanza is rendered in English both congruently and literally, line for line.

Apart from substitutions in non-key meaning, changes for the sake of congruence can involve replacing rhetorical figures, as long as the overall artistic effect does not suffer too much. The title of this book gives an example of converting a simile ("как соль на топоре", "like salt on an axe" – see p. 42) into a metaphor, "salt crystals on an axe", so that the result fits into the required metrical structure: ∪ -∪ -∪ -. The solution also spells out the crystals implied in the original, which is, in effect, the opposite to dropping "look back" in the previous example.

Preserving Individuality

The presence of a unique, identifiable poetic voice of the author was a necessary condition for his inclusion in the Anthology, and a determined attempt has been made to preserve this voice in translation. That has been our guiding principle in making various choices during the translation process, and in particular in reconciling the demands of meaning and form. In making these decisions we looked far beyond the poems included in the respective entry: a large selection, if not the whole available body, of each author's works has been considered in order to establish the writer's idiosyncrasies. A good example of how this approach works in practice is a decisively Mayakovskian rhyme introduced into the first two lines of 'The Brooklyn Bridge' on p. 55; the presence of a characteristic feature of the poetic voice of Vladimir Mayakovsky gives the English version a touch of authenticity despite the fact that the translation of these lines is far from literal (see note 6 on p. 64).

Other examples of preserving idiosyncrasies include the rare word "capsulets" in the last stanza on p. 103, which was chosen to translate the old-fashioned word облатки, and a Scots phrase on p. 269, which corresponds to a Ukrainianism occurring in the original.

The choice between British English, which is the norm in this book, and US English, which the translator has preferred in several cases, is also a reflection of the individual traits of some authors. US English was chosen when the author's poetic voice could be much better matched by the American vernacular and by its cultural milieu. We did our best not to mix the two linguistic standards in translations from the same poet.

We have generally preserved the visual characteristics of each poem: the layout and alignment of lines, the capitalisation, and the policy with respect to punctuation (the latter does not, of course, mean applying Russian conventions to English text). On very few occasions, when we felt that the readability of the translation could be impaired otherwise, we have used grammatical capitalisation and/or punctuation even though the author had made a different choice.

It is worth re-iterating that the English versions of all poems in the Anthology were produced by one and the same translator.

Whenever a reader of the translations can feel differences in style and manner, those are bound to be reflections of the genuine differences between the Russian poets rather than their translators.

The Principles of Selection

All poems in the present Anthology were written in the Russian language in the 20th century and can be described as mainstream, with a few arguably bordering on the avant-garde. We recognise avant-garde poetry, but believe that its interests are not best served by presenting it with mainstream works under the same cover.

Our goal was to provide an interesting and varied, rather than "representative", collection. The coverage of the massive corpus of 20th-century Russian poetry in a book of modest size inevitably has to be patchy; consequently, we aimed to capture at least some of the characteristic achievements, developments and flavours of the period. The decisions made were, of course, subjective and were moderated by the volume limitation and by the stance of some of the copyright holders. Nevertheless, we hope that we have offered a sufficient variety of good poetry to make the reader want to seek and read more.

We have given preference to shorter poems, the majority of which fit into one page; "mini" in the title of the book alludes to this principle. This is not unreasonable because of the traditional brevity of Russian verse; there is even a dedicated Russian word, стихотворение, meaning a short poem. Eight lines (two quatrains or four couplets) and twelve lines (three quatrains) have been signature formats of this poetic tradition since the 19th century. Virtually every Russian poet of note has written at least one fine 8-liner; it would have been entirely possible to put together an anthology in that format alone. In choosing shorter poems over longer ones we were also mindful of those readers who might want to learn some of the poems by heart, recite them at a school poetry-reading competition, etc. A certain number of longer poems were included to avoid a distortion of the overall picture; naturally, we gave that extra space to poets who excelled in longer forms.

Because of the nature of this Anthology, two additional constraints were imposed:

Translata-bility into English	Not a single piece was selected just because it would be easy to render it in English, and we hope that bilingual readers will appreciate the magnitude of the challenges that arose in translating some of the poems included. However, not everything lends itself to translation, especially when the scope of cultural context and the degree of inter-textuality exceed the efficacy of a few brief notes.[13]
Metrical verse only	*Vers libre* was excluded altogether, as our guiding principle of congruent translation is not applicable to it. The presence of rhyme was not a requirement, but we ended up selecting only six unrhymed poems for the Anthology (which is probably a fair reflection of the incidence of unrhymed verse in the corpus of 20th-century Russian poetry).

The following factors also played a part in selection:

Thematic and stylistic diversity	We tried to include poems that we felt could only be written by a Russian poet, but also those that could have been written anywhere in the world and some of those that did not at all look as if they were written by a Russian; poems invoking the shared European or Christian roots, but also works that are distinctly non-European. Special attention was given to inter-cultural themes.
Both the known and the unknown	We made an effort to choose a good number of works that, to the best of our knowledge, had never been published in English. At the same time, we felt that it was important to demonstrate the difference that congruent translation made, so we also included famous poems for which multiple translations had already existed.

Coverage of time periods	The frontispiece chart shows the authors' life spans.
The motif of the sky and heavenly bodies	It is ubiquitous in the book, starting with the title, and cropping up throughout the collection including the very first and last lines. It is in the habit of a Russian intellectual to look to the sky for philosophical and aesthetic stimulation as well as to regard it as a spiritual symbol; we used the same to help us hold a diverse collection together.

Restricting the size of each entry to two pieces, in line with the mini-anthology format, has allowed us to cover a good variety of poets while still showing the range of each individual author: in theme, form, tone or length. Vladimir Vishnevsky's entry (see p. 327) is an exception – made on the basis of extreme brevity of his preferred poetic form. Additional translations from Mandelstam and Blok appear in notes to other poets' entries.

Organisation of the Content

The entries are ordered by the author's date of birth; a bilingual index of poets is provided in the Appendix (pp. 370, 371). The order of poems within a single entry was decided in each case individually, and is not necessarily chronological. The year of writing is indicated where we felt that this information would assist the reader in understanding the context of the poem (see p. 127 for an example) or its place in the author's corpus: e.g. whether it was written particularly early or particularly late in his or her life, before or after imprisonment etc. Sometimes knowing the year of composition may help the reader to appreciate an artistic technique used in the piece: for example, the switch from past to present tense in the middle of the poem on p. 165 instantly spans a gap of over 50 years.

We decided against including biographic information, which is, in most cases, easily available elsewhere. The only exceptions are indication of the year of birth (and, where applicable, death) of the author and a footnote with the citation for Nobel Prize winners (pp. 9, 35, 265).

On the other hand, we have been reasonably generous with annotation, to aid deeper understanding of the poems and to avoid misleading the reader where the translator takes small liberties. The endnotes which follow most entries fall into the following categories:

- Background information for the readers who do not have sufficient knowledge of Russian realities and culture.
- Explanation of dedications and inter-textual references.
- Indication of significant changes to non-key meaning made to maintain congruence.
- Indication of deviations from congruence, giving the reasons for them (for example, note 2 on p. 104).
- Explanation of unusual or irregular language in the original. We have aimed to explain everything that may not be found in a medium-size dictionary.
- Notes on finer aspects of a poem that are likely to be overlooked by a casual reader.

Explanations that are not language-specific are generally given as notes to the translations rather than to the originals. Notes that relate to the whole poem are anchored to its title or to the first line if the poem is untitled.

The Appendix includes a concise chronology of 20th-century Russian history (pp. 358–365), to which the reader may wish to refer for the context of individual authors' lives. The poems that look somewhat cryptic are likely to become clearer when placed in the relevant historical perspective; the year of composition provided beneath a poem is often also an invitation to do just that.

Comparable Collections

Excepting the works marred by insufficient sensitivity to the originals, by extravagant usage of the target language or by apparent misunderstanding of the relevant prosodic concepts, we are aware of only a few anthologies of 20th-century Russian poetry in English translation where the poetic form of the originals has received systematic attention. Nearly all these collections were published in the 1950s and 60s, before the neglect of form in translation became widespread.

One is the book by Vladimir Markov and Merrill Sparks (1966); coincidentally, it also used only one translator. Markov and Sparks chose a compromise different from ours: they tried to stay very close to the meaning of the original and adjusted the form as required:

> From the very beginning, we rejected what seems a favourite procedure with some translators, namely, to convert the rhymed original written in an identifiable meter into English free verse. But in time we became convinced that trying to achieve precision cuts both ends ... If a sacrifice had to be made, we often sacrificed the rhyme. We dropped it, say, in odd-numbered lines or even omitted it entirely ... Sometimes we changed the original meter to avoid worse consequences ... In rare cases, we even had to resort to free verse while translating an original which has both meter and rhyme, as is the case with Steiger and some of Mandelstamm. (ibid. lxxix)

As a result, the majority of the translations in that collection are semi-congruent: a typical example would have only half of the lines rhymed, with a relaxed metre which is not far removed from that of the original. While this is a considerable improvement on the "favourite procedure with some translators", our "double injustice" argument (p. xliii) remains valid: this system demands real, very noticeable sacrifices in form in order to achieve equal accuracy in key and non-key meanings, while the need for such accuracy is at best debatable. In some cases it is not at all clear what was gained at the expense of the form: for example, the translation of "Insomnia. Homer. And sails drawn tight..." by Mandelstam (Markov and Sparks 1966: 291) does not appear, on the whole, more precise semantically than our fully congruent version "Insomnia. Greek verse. Taut canvas on display..." found on p. 41. Bearing in mind that the poem in question addresses the *Iliad*, abandoning the hexameter (albeit iambic rather than dactylic) can hardly be described as an insignificant loss. This can also be said about dropping the rhymes: Mandelstam was no stranger to blank verse; if he chose to rhyme this poem, he must have had a reason.[14]

Another anthology that paid serious attention to form was put together by Jack Lindsay (1957). Again, only one translator was involved. Lindsay generally translated fully rhymed poems as fully rhymed, but his attitude towards metre was even more liberal than that of Markov and Sparks:

The versions are line for line and keep to the general stanzaic form of the original; I do not however attempt the beat-for-beat exactitude in metre in view of certain differences in the structure and texture of Russian and English. Russian for one thing with its assonantal systems can use double-rhymes as English cannot. (ibid. xxii)

In the small follow-up collection (1960) Lindsay was prepared to go as far as radically altering the stanzaic form and the rhyme scheme of a piece: his version of Mandelstam's 'Leningrad' (ibid. 24) renders the seven rhymed couplets as an English sonnet, rhymed and laid out as *abab cdcd effe gg*. At the same time, the anapaestic tetrameter of the original becomes accentual verse leaning towards, and in the last two lines turning into, iambic pentameter. Our translation of this poem appears, interleaved with the original text, on p. xxxix, where it is used to demonstrate a technique of validating congruence.

Two anthologies published in Russia – (Ognev and Rottenberg 1969) and (Kupriyanova and Ivanovskaya 1981) – consist of works by many translators who did not adhere to any shared set of principles. Nevertheless, the majority of translations included in these books reflect the form of the originals. Avril Pyman, Dorian Rottenberg, Peter Tempest and Louis Zellikoff are in some cases quite close to our system in the way they deal with the compromises involved in preserving metre and rhyme. For instance, Dorian Rottenberg largely reproduced the amphibrach of 'Parabolical Ballad' by Andrey Voznesensky (Ognev and Rottenberg 1969: 131–133) and also came up with a mosaic rhyme "gravity"-"have at him", which is very much in the spirit of the original (where the corresponding rhyme is actually conventional and feminine rather than dactylic). The penultimate line of Peter Tempest's translation of the introductory poem from *Cinematograph* by Semyon Kirsanov (Kupriyanova and Ivanovskaya 1981: 80) contains an example of using a diphthong to render a feminine caesura.

A broader comparison should include collections without an editorial policy on the preservation of form in translation. The table that follows provides some idea as to the content of *Salt Crystal on an Axe* (*SCA*) in contrast to 26 other anthologies, identified by their ordinal numbers in the References section and ordered by the number of authors shared with *SCA*.

Reference number	Year of first publication	Attention to form	Bilingual or English only	Authors in total	Authors shared with SCA	Poems shared with SCA	New authors in SCA	New poems in SCA
57	'93	some	E	245	46	12	10	108
15	'92	some	E	82	27	5	29	115
14	'78	some	E	73	(earlier edition of No 15)			
30	'66	yes	B	87	20	8	36	112
36	'65	no	B	35*	15	6	41	114
55	'74	some	E	26	15	3	41	117
11	'72	some	E	20	14	4	42	116
53	'09	some	E	20†	14	0	42	120
25	'06	no	B	24‡	13	6	43	114
24	'81	yes	E	63	13	2	43	118
48	'93	no	B	23	13	1	43	119
10	'69	some	B	15	12	6	44	114
37	'69	yes	B	33§	12	0	44	120
12	'84	no	E	16	11	2	45	118
20	'97	some	B	32	11	0	45	120
45	'68	no	B	17	9	1	47	119
9	'08	some	B	44	9	0	47	120
31	'85	some	E	10	7	3	49	117
29	'60	yes	E	21	7	1	49	119

* Excluding the pre-20th-century authors.
† Excluding the 19th-century authors.
‡ Excluding the 18th- and 19th-century authors.
§ Excluding the authors who wrote in languages other than Russian.

Reference number	Year of first publication	Attention to form	Bilingual or English only	Authors in total	Authors shared with SCA	Poems shared with SCA	New authors in SCA	New poems in SCA
18	'00	no	E	85	7	1	49	119
28	'57	yes	E	33	6	0	50	120
19	'92	no	E	21	6	0	50	120
26	'73	some	B	25	4	0	52	120
35	'08	some	B	4*	4	0	52	120
32	'03	no	E	10	3	1	53	119
23	'06	n/a†	B	20	3	0	53	120

---

* Excluding the 18th- and 19th-century authors.
† Mainly free-verse originals.

References

1   APPEL, ALFRED JR. and NABOKOV, VLADIMIR (1967). 'An Interview with Vladimir Nabokov'. *Wisconsin Studies in Contemporary Literature*, 8/2, A Special Number Devoted to Vladimir Nabokov, Spring.

2   ARNDT, WALTER (1972). *Pushkin Threefold: The Originals with Linear and Metric Translations*. London: Allen & U.

3   BARNSTONE, WILLIS (1993). *The Poetics of Translation: History, Theory, Practice*. Yale University Press.

4   BRODSKY, JOSEPH (1986). 'The Child of Civilization'. In *Less than One: Selected Essays*. New York: Farrar, Straus and Giroux.

5   BRODSKY, JOSEPH (2001a). *Collected Poems in English*. New York: Farrar, Straus and Giroux.

6   BRODSKY, JOSEPH (2001b). *Nativity Poems*. New York: Farrar, Straus and Giroux.

7   BRODSKY, JOSEPH; MAXWELL, GLYN, trans. (2004). 'A Letter to General Z.'. *New Yorker*, October 4th.

8   BRODSKY, JOSEPH, comp.; MYERS, ALAN, trans. (1988). *An Age Ago: A Selection of Nineteenth-Century Russian Poetry*. New York: Farrar, Straus and Giroux.

9   BUNIMOVICH, EVGENY, ed.; KATES, J., trans. ed. (2008). *Contemporary Russian Poetry: An Anthology*. Urbana-Champaign, IL: Dalkey Archive Press.

10 CARLISLE, OLGA, comp. and ed. (1970). *Poets on Street Corners: Portraits of Fifteen Russian Poets*. New York: Vintage.

11 CARLISLE, OLGA and STYRON, ROSE, eds. and trans. (1972). *Modern Russian Poetry*. New York: Viking Press.

12 FORD, R.A.D., comp. and trans. (1987). *Russian Poetry: A Personal Anthology*. Oakville, Ontario: Mosaic Press.

13 FRY, STEPHEN (2005). *The Ode Less Travelled: Unlocking a Poet Within*. London: Hutchinson.

14 GLAD, JOHN and WEISSBORT, DANIEL, eds. (1978). *Russian Poetry: The Modern Period*. University of Iowa Press.

15 GLAD, JOHN and WEISSBORT, DANIEL, eds. (1992). *Twentieth Century Russian Poetry*. University of Iowa Press.

16 HEANEY, SEAMUS and HASS, ROBERT (2000). 'Sounding Lines: The Art of Translating Poetry', Doreen B. Townsend Center Occasional Papers, year 1999, paper 20. University of California.

17 HEWLETT, HENRY G (1891). 'Rhyme and Reason in English Verse'. *Library*, s1–3.

18 HIGH, JOHN, ed. (2000). *Crossing Centuries: The New Russian Poetry*. Jersey City, NJ: Talisman House.

19 JOHNSON, KENT and ASHBY, STEPHEN M., eds. (1992). *Third Wave: The New Russian Poetry*. University of Michigan Press.

20 KATES, J., ed. (1999). *In the Grip of Strange Thoughts: Russian Poetry in a New Era*. Brookline, MA: Zephyr Press.

21 KIBIROV, TIMUR (1995). Кибиров Тимур. Когда был Ленин маленьким. СПб.: Издательство Ивана Лимбаха.

22 KLINE, GEORGE L. (1994). 'Seven by Ten: An Examination of Seven Pairs of Translations from Akhmatova by Ten English and American Translators'. *The Slavic and East European Journal*, 38/1, Spring.

23 KUDRYAVITSKY, ANATOLY, trans. and ed. (2006). *A Night in the Nabokov Hotel: 20 Contemporary Poets from Russia*. Dublin: Dedalus Press.

24 KUPRIYANOVA, NINA and IVANOVSKAYA, ARIADNA, comps. (1981). *Soviet Russian Poetry of the 1950s–1970s*. Moscow: Progress.

25 KUTIK, ILYA and WACHTEL, ANDREW, eds. *From the Ends to the Beginning: A Bilingual Anthology of Russian Verse* [online, ongoing project]. Department of Slavic Languages and Literatures, Northwestern University. <www.russianpoetry.net> [cited 17 December 2006].

26 LANGLAND, JOSEPH, ACZEL, TAMAS and TIKOS, LASZLO, trans. and eds. (1973). *Poetry from the Russian Underground: A Bilingual Anthology*. New York: Harper & Row.

27 LERMONTOV, M.IU.; LIBERMAN, ANATOLY, trans. and ed. (1984). *Major Poetry*. London: Croom Helm.

28 LINDSAY, JACK, comp. and trans. (1957). *Russian Poetry, 1917–1955*. London: Bodley Head.

29 LINDSAY, JACK, comp. and trans. (1960). *Modern Russian Poetry*. London: Vista Books.

30 MARKOV, VLADIMIR and SPARKS, MERRILL, eds. (1966). *Modern Russian Poetry: An Anthology with Verse Translations*. London: MacGibbon & Kee.

31 MCKANE, RICHARD, comp and trans. (1990). *20th Century Russian Poetry*. London: Kozmik Press.

32 MCKANE, RICHARD, ed. (2003). *Ten Russian Poets*. London: Anvil Press Poetry.

33 NABOKOV, VLADIMIR (1964). *Notes on Prosody and Abram Gannibal: From the Commentary to the Author's Translation of Pushkin's Eugene Onegin*, Bollingen Series. Princeton University Press.

34 NABOKOV, VLADIMIR; SCAMMELL, MICHAEL, tr. (2001). *The Gift*, Penguin Classics. London: Penguin.

35 NABOKOV, VLADIMIR, comp. and trans.; BOYD, BRIAN and SHVABRIN, STANISLAV, eds. (2008). *Verses and Versions: Three Centuries of Russian Poetry*. Orlando, FL: Harcourt.

36 OBOLENSKY, DMITRI, ed. (1976). *The Heritage of Russian Verse*. Indiana University Press.

37 OGNEV, VLADIMIR and ROTTENBERG, DORIAN, comps. (1969). *Fifty Soviet Poets*. Moscow: Progress.

38 PETERSON, NADYA L. (1995). 'Contemporary Russian Poetry: A Bilingual Anthology, by Gerald S. Smith'. *Slavic Review*, 54/1, Spring.

39 PUSHKIN, A.S.; ARNDT, WALTER, trans. (1981). *Eugene Onegin: A Novel in Verse: Second Edition, Revised*. New York: Dutton.

40 PUSHKIN, A.S.; FALEN, JAMES E., trans. (1998). *Eugene Onegin: A Novel in Verse*, Oxford World's Classics. Oxford University Press.

41 PUSHKIN, A.S.; HOFSTADTER, DOUGLAS R., trans. (2000). *Eugene Onegin: A Novel in Verse*. New York: Basic Books.

42 PUSHKIN, A.S.; JOHNSTON, SIR CHARLES, trans. (1979). *Eugene Onegin: A Novel in Verse*, Penguin Classics. London: Penguin.

43 PUSHKIN, A.S.; MITCHELL, STANLEY, trans. (2008). *Eugene Onegin: A Novel in Verse*, Penguin Classics. London: Penguin.

44 PUSHKIN, ALEXANDER; LIEUT.-COL. SPALDING, H., trans. (1881). *Eugene Oneguine: A Romance of Russian Life in Verse*. London: Macmillan and Co.

45   REAVEY, GEORGE, comp., ed. and trans. (1981). *The New Russian Poets 1953–68: An Anthology.* London: Marion Boyars.

46   SCHERR, BARRY P. (1986). *Russian Poetry: Meter, Rhythm, and Rhyme.* University of California Press.

47   SETH, VIKRAM (1986). *The Golden Gate.* New York: Random House.

48   SMITH, GERALD S., comp., ed. and trans. (1993). *Contemporary Russian Poetry: A Bilingual Anthology.* Indiana University Press.

49   STEELE, TIMOTHY (1999). *All the Fun's in How You Say a Thing: An Explanation of Meter and Versification.* Ohio University Press.

50   SZIRTES, GEORGE (2006). 'Formal Wear: Notes on Rhyme, Meter, Stanza & Pattern'. *Poetry*, 187/5, February.

51   TYUTCHEV, F.I.; BATALDEN, STEVEN K. and NOONAN, THOMAS, eds.; LIBERMAN, ANATOLY, trans. (1993). *On the Heights of Creation: Lyrics.* Stamford, CT: JAI Press.

52   WACHTEL, MICHAEL (1998). *The Development of Russian Verse: Meter and its Meanings*, Cambridge Studies in Russian Literature. Cambridge University Press.

53   WASHINGTON, PETER, ed. (2009). *Russian Poets*, Everyman's Library Pocket Poets. New York: Alfred A. Knopf.

54   WEBSTER, DANIEL (2001). 'Insomnia and Homer: A Comparative Study of Translations into English of an Early Poem by Osip Mandelstam'. *Translation Review*, 60.

55   WEISSBORT, DANIEL, ed. (1974). *Post-War Russian Poetry.* Harmondsworth, Middlesex: Penguin.

56   WEISSBORT, DANIEL (2002). 'Something Like His Own Language'. *Notre Dame Review*, 14.

57   YEVTUSHENKO, YEVGENY, comp.; TODD, ALBERT and HAYWARD, MAX, eds. (1993). *Twentieth Century Russian Poetry: Silver and Steel: An Anthology.* New York: Doubleday.

Notes

1 In a case of life imitating art, Suleimenov served as Kazakhstan's ambassador to Italy many years later.

2 Interestingly, in our recent telephone conversation with Yevtushenko he remarked that he did not believe in the feasibility of rendering Russian rhymes in English. That, of course, does not diminish the truth of the quotation: the "music" in question is the overall harmony of a spoken poetic word.

3 This is not to say that every single translation contained in these anthologies completely ignores the form of the original. Daniel Weissbort, for example, occasionally retains some aspects of the form in his own translations from Russian included in the anthologies edited by him.

4 There have, of course, been exceptions from this general rule. The bilingual anthology of contemporary Russian poetry compiled and translated by Anatoly Kudryavitsky (2006) is an example of a collection where the absence of metre and rhyme must have been an important selection criterion, even though it was not declared as such by the compiler.

5 This mapping is less trivial than it may seem: *dolnik* is relaxed syllabic-accentual verse, based on lexical stress while "English *dolnik*" is disciplined accentual verse, based on phrasal or syntagmatic stress.

6 A good example is given by the two poems in Alexander Kushner's entry (pp. 226, 228): they are very different rhythmically despite being written in the same metre and having the same placement of rhymes. The difference is to a large extent due to the pattern of masculine and feminine endings: *AAbCCb* vs *aaBccB*.

7 Here is Vladimir Nabokov's strident description (Nabokov, Boyd and Shvabrin 2008: 12) of the plight of a translator of rhymed poetry into English:

> It is not the head of the verse line that'll
> Cause him trouble, nor it is the spine:
> What he really minds is the cursed rattle
> That must be found for the tail of the line.

8 Nabokov once mentioned "a certain subdued and delicate beauty of gray, gentle rhyme in English" (1964: 85).

[9] (Pushkin and Spalding 1881) is yet another example, albeit mainly of curiosity value. It is also apparently the earliest ever English translation of *Onegin*.

[10] The translations found in this collection, including Richard Wilbur's translation of 'Шесть лет спустя' mentioned on p. xlv, carry the approval of the Estate of Joseph Brodsky who requested that we make this fact clear to our readers.

[11] Walter Arndt once described (1972: xxviii) the literalistic approach evangelised by Nabokov as "sad ritual murder performed for the purposes of an ever more insatiable lexical necrophilia". However, Nabokov did not always adhere to this extreme position. Some of the self-translations of the poems incorporated into his novel *The Gift*, including that of the epilogic piece (2001: 333) written in the *Onegin* stanza, are excellent examples of congruent translation. Nabokov's self-translations contributed to the anthology by Markov and Sparks (1966: 479) are near-congruent. In (Nabokov, Boyd and Shvabrin 2008) one also occasionally encounters translations that deploy "arty paraphrase" to preserve or approximate the form of the original.

The strength of feelings about this matter appears undiminished 30 years after Nabokov's death: we have been unable to secure permission from the Nabokov Estate to include our congruent translations of his poems 'Мать' (Mother) and "Мы с тобою так верили в связь бытия..." (You and I so believed in the linkage of being...) in this Anthology.

[12] An interesting question arising in this respect is whether the crib writer can possibly guess what fine points, linguistic, cultural or literary, may turn out to be relevant and hence need to be explained to the translator. The conventional wisdom, much upheld by publishers, is that any translation should be done into the translator's mother tongue. However, it may well be the case that Russian poetry should be translated by people whose knowledge of the Russian language, culture and literature is at least as good as their command of English; failing that, perhaps a bilingual editor who fits that description should be kept in the loop as the translation is repeatedly revised.

[13] An extreme example is given by Chapter IV of Timur Kibirov's (1995) poem 'Когда был Ленин маленьким' (When Lenin Was a Little Boy). There is roughly one intertextual reference per line there, and although Anglophone readers may be able to pick up some of them (to Greek myths, Catullus, Coleridge, Baudelaire, Poe), the chapter is

full of references to Russian literature of three centuries, Russian folklore and Soviet popular culture. They cannot possibly be understood by readers who need a translation; in fact, many of today's educated native speakers of Russian would find some of these references obscure. Nevertheless, a translation has been published (Johnson and Ashby 1992: 228–229), and it does not offer any explanatory notes whatsoever.

[14] Daniel Webster (2001) discusses five other translations of this poem, including his own. Many more translations of it have been published.

SALT CRYSTALS ON AN AXE

Through the pallid window pane

сквозь бледное окно

Иннокентий Анненский

1855—1909

Среди миров

Среди миров, в мерцании светил
Одной Звезды я повторяю имя...
Не потому, чтоб я Ее любил,
А потому, что я томлюсь с другими.

И если мне сомненье тяжело,
Я у Нее одной ищу ответа,
Не потому, что от Нее светло,
А потому, что с Ней не надо света.

Innokenty Annensky

1855–1909

'Midst Stellar Worlds

'Midst stellar worlds and twinkling lights galore
I call one Star across the boundless aether.
It's not because she's one that I'd adore,
But that I'm ill at ease with any other.

And if I doubt then doubts shall be my plight
Until a word from her is sought and heeded.
It's not because her light is shining bright:
When I'm with her, no light is ever needed.

Сиреневая мгла

Наша улица снегами залегла,
По снегам бежит сиреневая мгла.

Мимоходом только глянула в окно,
И я понял, что люблю ее давно.

Я молил ее, сиреневую мглу:
«Погости-побудь со мной в моем углу,

Не мою тоску ты давнюю развей,
Поделись со мной, желанная, своей!»

Но лишь издали услышал я в ответ:
«Если любишь, так и сам отыщешь след.

Где над омутом синеет тонкий лед,
Там часочек погощу я, кончив лет,

А у печки-то никто нас не видал...
Только те мои, кто волен да удал.»

LILAC MIST

Heavy snows have turned our street into a piste,
Down the snow crust glides a beauty, Lilac Mist.

Her quick glance into the window is enough
For my heart to recognise it is in love.

And I beg of her: "My precious Lilac Mist,
Come and stay with me inside my chamber triste.

I'm not asking that my misery you quell.
What is yours, oh my beloved one, pray tell?"

And I hear a quiet answer down the dale:
"If you love me, by yourself you'll find my trail.

Where blue ice is thinly covering a lake
I will end the flight and then my time I'll take.

Me in chambers – not a soul could ever see…
Only those are mine, whose hearts are bold and free."

Иван Бунин

1870—1953

ВОСКРЕСЕНИЕ

В апрельский жаркий полдень, по кремнистой
Дороге меж цветущими садами
Пришел монах, высокий францисканец,
К монастырю над синим южным морем.
«Кто там?» — сказал Привратник из-за двери.
«Брат во Христе», — ответил францисканец.
«Кого вам надо?» — «Брата Габриэля».
«Он нынче занят — пишет Воскресенье».
Тогда монах сорвал с ограды розу,
Швырнул во двор — и с недовольным видом
Пошел назад. А роза за оградой
Рассыпалась на мрамор черным пеплом.

Ivan Bunin

1870–1953

RESURRECTION

One scorching April day, a tall Franciscan
Came walking up a stony winding road
Which ran along resplendent flowering gardens
Up to a cloister by a southern seashore.
"Who's there?" the Guard asked from behind the portal.
"A brother in the Lord", said the Franciscan.
"Who are you after?" "Brother Gabrielë".
"He's busy: has to paint the Resurrection".
The stranger plucked a rosebud from the trellis
And flung it over with exasperation,
And back he went. While in the yard the rosebud
Over the marble scattered in black ashes.

Laureate of the Nobel Prize in Literature: 1933, "for the strict artistry with which he has carried on the classical Russian traditions in prose writing".

* * *

И цветы, и шмели, и трава, и колосья,
И лазурь, и полуденный зной...
Срок настанет — господь сына блудного спросит:
«Был ли счастлив ты в жизни земной?»

И забуду я все — вспомню только вот эти
Полевые пути меж колосьев и трав —
И от сладостных слез не успею ответить,
К милосердным коленям припав.

* * *

Summer blooms, bumblebees, ears of wheat, stacks of threshed hay,
Midday heat and the sky's azure light...
There'll be time for the prodigal son to be questioned;
God will ask: "Wast thou happy in life?"

I'll forget many things, but this much I'll remember:
Footpaths laid across fields full of grass and grain ears...
And in sweet tears of bliss to my Lord I'll surrender,
Clinging, mute, to His merciful knees.

Александр Блок

1880—1921

* * *

В густой траве пропадешь с головой.
В тихий дом войдешь, не стучась...
Обнимет рукой, оплетет косой
И, статная, скажет: «Здравствуй, князь.

Вот здесь у меня — куст белых роз.
Вот здесь вчера — повилика вилась.
Где был, пропадал? что за весть принес?
Кто любит, не любит, кто гонит нас?»

Как бывало, забудешь, что дни идут,
Как бывало, простишь, кто горд и зол.
И смотришь — тучи вдали встают,
И слушаешь песни далеких сел...

Заплачет сердце по чужой стороне,
Запросится в бой — зовет и мани́т...
Только скажет: «Прощай. Вернись ко мне» —
И опять за травой колокольчик звенит...

Alexander Blok

1880–1921

* * *

The grass was dense, covering head-high,[1]
Not a knock, you stepped through the fence…
Her arm would embrace and her plait would tie,
Gay and stately, she'd say: "Hail, prince".

"Here – look! – I have grown a snow-white rose;
Here a few days back a dodder climbed.
Just where have you been, what news have brought?
Who troubles us, who dislikes, who likes?"

You'd forget again that days zoomed by,
You'd forgive again people's pride and wrongs,
And watch far-away rain clouds loom high,
And listen to distant hamlets' songs…

Your heart would miss the thrill of attack,
And a stranger land would pluck its strings.
She would only say "Fare you well. Come back."
And again through the grass the bell would ring.

* * *

Седые сумерки легли
Весной на город бледный.
Автомобиль пропел вдали
В рожок победный.

Глядись сквозь бледное окно,[2]
К стеклу прижавшись плотно...
Глядись. Ты изменил давно,
Бесповоротно.

* * *

A hoary dusk, the day adjourned.
Spring and a city pallid.[3]
Hoots from a passing motor horn
Triumphed and dallied.

Look through the pallid window pane,
The glass reflecting glances.
Your self-betrayal. The old bane.
No second chances.

Notes

[1] The metre of the original is a 4-beat *dolnik*.

[2] The seemingly illogical combination of the verb глядеться (to look at oneself), which strongly suggests a mirror and takes the preposition в (in), with the preposition сквозь (through) is suggestive of the dawn light when it is possible to look through the window glass at the city beyond and see one's reflection in that glass at the same time.

[3] St Petersburg.

The catalogue of ships

список кораблей

Николай Гумилев

1886—1921

ЖИРАФ

Сегодня, я вижу, особенно грустен твой взгляд
И руки особенно то́нки, колени обняв.
Послушай: далёко, далёко, на озере Чад
    Изысканный бродит жираф.

Ему грациозная стройность и нега дана,
И шкуру его украшает волшебный узор,
С которым равняться осмелится только луна,
Дробясь и качаясь на влаге широких озер.

Вдали он подобен цветным парусам корабля,
И бег его плавен, как радостный птичий полет.
Я знаю, что много чудесного видит земля,
Когда на закате он прячется в мраморный грот.

Я знаю веселые сказки таинственных стран
Про черную деву, про страсть молодого вождя,
Но ты слишком долго вдыхала тяжелый туман,
Ты верить не хочешь во что-нибудь, кроме дождя.

И как я тебе расскажу про тропический сад,
Про стройные пальмы, про запах немыслимых трав...
— Ты плачешь? Послушай... далёко, на озере Чад
    Изысканный бродит жираф.

Nikolai Gumilyov

1886–1921

GIRAFFE

I see that this morning your eyes are unusually sad.
Your arms look especially thin as your knees they enwrap.[1]
I say, overseas – a great distance away – by Lake Chad
    There saunters a dainty giraffe.

He's slender and graceful, and blessed with contentment and flair.
His hide is adorned with a magical pattern ornate,
With which only rays of the Moon ever dare to compare
When she splits and bobs on the ripples of wide open lakes.

He looks, from afar, like the colourful sails of a boat,
His gait smooth and steady, as would be a bird's joyous flight.
I know: many wonders are seen by his marble abode,
When into a grotto he hurries to hide for the night.

I keep in my mind some mysterious tribe's jocund tales:
About a black virgin, about a young chieftain's heart call,
But since for too long heavy fog has been all you inhaled
You wouldn't believe anything, anything but rainfall.

So how will I tell you about that great tropical land,
The tall slender palm trees, the smell of incredible grass?[2]
– You're crying? I say... a great distance away, by Lake Chad
    There saunters a dainty giraffe.

СТАРЫЙ КОНКВИСТАДОР [3]

Углубясь в неведомые горы,
Заблудился старый конквиста́дор,
В дымном небе плавали кондо́ры,[4]
Нависали снежные громады.

Восемь дней скитался он без пищи,
Конь издох, но под большим уступом
Он нашел уютное жилище,
Чтоб не разлучаться с милым трупом.

Там он жил в тени сухих смоковниц,
Песни пел о солнечной Кастилье,
Вспоминал сраженья и любовниц,
Видел то пищали, то мантильи.

Как всегда, был дерзок и спокоен
И не знал ни ужаса, ни злости,
Смерть пришла, и предложил ей воин
Поиграть в изломанные кости.

Old Conquistador

Wand'ring deep into untrodden mountains,
The conquistador had lost his bearings.
Condors soared. The sky whipped smoky cloud stains.
Snowy ledges loomed, tremendous, therein.

For a week he wandered gaunt and hungry,
Saw his horse drop dead beside a crevice.
So he found a place to live in comfort,
Close to where the cherished corpse was buried.

There he lived 'neath desiccated branches
Singing sunny songs about Castilla.
He recalled his battles and his wenches,
Seeing in turn the guns and the mantillas.

He was always daring, calm and offhand;
Felt no wrath, and fright could not accost him.
Death arrived, and this old soldier offered
Battered dice to him, and asked to toss them.

Notes

[1] The poem was addressed to Anna Akhmatova.

[2] Gumilyov travelled to Africa and hunted lions there.

[3] This is an old-fashioned spelling of the word конкистадо́р; the normative stress, in both versions, is as indicated in this note.

[4] The normative stress is ко́ндор. It was a freshly borrowed foreign word in the Russian language of the early 20th century, and it was likely to have been known to Gumilyov from a French source; hence the end-stress characteristic of the Russian perception of French words.

Владислав Ходасевич

1886—1939

* * *

Перешагни, перескочи,
Перелети, пере- что хочешь —
Но вырвись: камнем из пращи,
Звездой, сорвавшейся в ночи́...
Сам затерял — теперь ищи...

Бог знает, что себе бормочешь,
Ища пенсне или ключи.

Vladislav Khodasevich

1886–1939

* * *

Step over this, bound forth, or lunge
Across, but, damn it, move it over.
Break out: as does a stone when slung,
A star at night that takes the plunge…
You lost it – find it, that's the crunch.

Good Lord, the words one mutters over
Locating keys, a missing bunch!

ПУТЕМ ЗЕРНА

Проходит сеятель по ровным бороздам.
Отец его и дед по тем же шли путям.

Сверкает золотом в его руке зерно,
Но в землю черную оно упасть должно.

И там, где червь слепой прокладывает ход,
Оно в заветный срок умрет и прорастет.

Так и душа моя идет путем зерна:
Сойдя во мрак, умрет — и оживет она.

И ты, моя страна, и ты, ее народ,
Умрешь и оживешь, пройдя сквозь этот год, —

Затем, что мудрость нам единая дана:
Всему живущему идти путем зерна.

1917

Vladislav Khodasevich

THE PATH OF GRAIN

The farmer walks along the furrows by a swath;
And generations back his fathers walked this path.

Though grain is shiny gold when lying in his hand,
When cast, into the dark of soil it has to land.

And there, where sightless worms' long burrows are being made,
It will, in proper time, pass on and germinate.

Thus will my very soul, which walks the path of grain,
Descend into the dark to die and rise again.

And you, my native land, and you, its people proud,
Will die and rise again, after this year is out.

The truth supreme before mankind has always lain:
That all that is alive shall walk the path of grain.

1917

Анна Ахматова

1889—1966

Последний тост

Я пью за разоренный дом,
За злую жизнь мою,
За одиночество вдвоем,
И за тебя я пью, —
За ложь меня предавших губ,
За мертвый холод глаз,
За то, что мир жесток и груб,
За то, что Бог не спас.

Anna Akhmatova

1889–1966

The Last Toast

I toast this devastated home,
I toast my wretched days
And solitude in coupledom;
To you my glass I raise –
To treason on your lying lips,
Your eyes of lifeless calm,
The callous world that's full of tricks,
And God's forsaking palm.

ПРИМОРСКИЙ СОНЕТ

Здесь всё меня переживет,
Всё, даже ветхие скворешни
И этот воздух, воздух вешний,
Морской свершивший перелет.

И голос вечности зовет
С неодолимостью нездешней,
И над цветущею черешней
Сиянье легкий месяц льет.

И кажется такой нетрудной,
Белея в чаще изумрудной,
Дорога не скажу куда...

Там средь стволов еще светлее,
И всё похоже на аллею
У царскосельского пруда.

1958

SEASIDE SONNET

All will remain when I'm no more,
Even the shabby old birdhouse;
Even this air, which from the south
Sailed here with spring and came ashore.

The calling voice of Evermore
Is otherworldly, hard to oust;
Into the cherry-blossom mouths
Rays of the weightless crescent pour.

The path across the emerald forest,
A milky glimmer through the foliage,
Seems easy – guess where it would go...[1]

Among the trunks the night is brighter
And all looks like the allée right by
The pond in Tsárskoye Seló.[2]

1958

Notes

[1] It goes to the cemetery of the seaside village of Komarovo on the Karelian Isthmus where Akhmatova had a modest dacha ("будка", "the Booth"). Her frequent walks to the cemetery were reported to the authorities by an informer: "Такое впечатление, что подыскивает место для себя" (this gives the impression that she is looking for a place for herself). This is exactly how it all ended; according to Archpriest Mikhail Ardov, Komarovo cemetery was chosen as the burial place for Akhmatova in part because it was featured in 'Seaside Sonnet'.

[2] Tsarskoye Selo (Царское Село, literally: "Tsar's village") is a town on the outskirts of St Petersburg with a palace and a park complex which served as a summer residence of the imperial family. Akhmatova lived there in her childhood and youth.

Tsarskoye Selo has a special significance for Russian culture, not least because Pushkin was educated in the Lycée located there, next to the palace. Innokenty Annensky, the poet whose entry opens this anthology, taught classical languages at a gymnasium in Tsarskoye Selo a century later; Nikolai Gumilyov – yet another poet included in this collection and Anna Akhmatova's first husband – was amongst his pupils.

Борис Пастернак

1890—1960

Гамлет

Гул затих. Я вышел на подмостки.
Прислонясь к дверному косяку,
Я ловлю в далеком отголоске,
Что случится на моем веку.

На меня наставлен сумрак ночи
Тысячью биноклей на оси.
Если только можно, Авва Отче,
Чашу эту мимо пронеси.

Я люблю твой замысел упрямый
И играть согласен эту роль.
Но сейчас идет другая драма,
И на этот раз меня уволь.

Но продуман распорядок действий,
И неотвратим конец пути.
Я один, всё тонет в фарисействе.
Жизнь прожить — не поле перейти.

Boris Pasternak

1890–1960

HAMLET [1]

Silence falls. I tread the boards, walk out.
Propped against the door, I stand upright,
Catching in a faint reflected sound
Signs of what is destined to betide.

Thrust against me is the night's dark stare,
Theatre-binocular array.
Abba, Father, all is in your care,
Take this cup away from me, I pray. [2]

You're a stubborn, formidable planner
And this role is fine for me to act,
But they've put on stage a different drama
And I wish my contract you'd retract.

Yet the list of acts has been laid out
And the path still ends, do what you may.
I'm alone with Pharisees around.
Life was never meant to be a play. [3]

Laureate of the Nobel Prize in Literature: 1958, "for his important achievement both in contemporary lyrical poetry and in the field of the great Russian epic tradition".

Зимняя ночь

Мело, мело по всей земле
Во все пределы.
Свеча горела на столе,
Свеча горела.

Как летом роем мошкара
Летит на пламя,
Слетались хлопья со двора
К оконной раме.

Метель лепила на стекле
Кружки и стрелы.
Свеча горела на столе,
Свеча горела.

На озаренный потолок
Ложились тени,
Скрещенья рук, скрещенья ног,
Судьбы скрещенья.

И падали два башмачка
Со стуком на пол.
И воск слезами с ночника
На платье капал.

И всё терялось в снежной мгле
Седой и белой.
Свеча горела на столе,
Свеча горела.

На свечку дуло из угла,
И жар соблазна
Вздымал, как ангел, два крыла
Крестообразно.

Мело весь месяц в феврале,
И то и дело
Свеча горела на столе,
Свеча горела.

Winter Night

The blizzard closed its cold white clench
The wide world o'er.
A candle glowed upon the bench,
A candle glowed.

In summertime mosquito swarms
Flew into fire,
And now the snowflakes – frozen throngs –
Were likewise flying.

A pattern on the pane was etched
By whirling snow.
The candle glowed upon the bench
The candle glowed.

Over the lit-up ceiling lay
Shadowy postings:
The crossings of the arms and legs,
The fateful crossings.

Then shoes dropped off, their double knock
Was loud and clear.
The candle shed onto the frock
Its waxen tear.

And all dissolved in that snow-drenched,
White, hoary flow.
The candle glowed upon the bench,
The candle glowed.

The draft would breathe over the wick.
The ghost of passion
Would, like an angel, raise its wings
In a cross fashion.

A month-long blizzard turned its wrench
And, oft and o'er,
A candle glowed upon the bench,
A candle glowed.

Notes

[1] Both poems by Pasternak selected for the anthology belong to the cycle 'Стихотворения Юрия Живаго' (The Poems of Yuri Zhivago) which forms part of his novel *Доктор Живаго* (*Doctor Zhivago*).

[2] The order of words differs from Mark 14: 36 (take away this cup from me), to reflect a similar change made in the original: "чашу эту мимо пронеси" instead of "пронеси чашу сию мимо Меня".

[3] The whole final line of the original is a Russian proverb which contrasts living one's life with walking across a field; its standard interpretation is "life was never meant to be easy". The choice of the word "play" (used in two meanings) in the translation of this line is justified by the multi-layered extended metaphor of life as a theatrical play which underpins the poem. Hamlet is acting insane and is being watched by everybody in Elsinore; the actor is playing a demanding role and is being watched by the audience; Pasternak is reflecting on his life while writing on behalf of his character Zhivago, who is reflecting on his. The identification with both Hamlet and the actor is strengthened by the fact that the play (which has another play performed within it) is presumably being staged in Pasternak's own controversial translation into Russian.

Осип Мандельштам

1891—1938

* * *

Бессонница. Гомер. Тугие паруса.
Я список кораблей прочел до середины:
Сей длинный выводок, сей поезд журавлиный,[1]
Что над Элладою когда-то поднялся.

Как журавлиный клин в чужие рубежи, —
На головах царей божественная пена, —
Куда плывете вы? Когда бы не Елена,
Что Троя вам одна, ахейские мужи?

И море, и Гомер — всё движется любовью.
Кого же слушать мне? И вот Гомер молчит,
И море черное, витийствуя, шумит [2]
И с тяжким грохотом подходит к изголовью.

1915

Osip Mandelstam

1891–1938

* * *

Insomnia. Greek verse. Taut canvas on display.
I've read the catalogue of ships down to the middle: [3]
This lengthy brood of cranes, this stretched formation regal
That in long past rose over Hellas on its way.

A siege of cranes in search of distant foreign lands,[4]
The foam of gods anoints the leaders of a nation.
Had Helen never lived, what'd be your destination?
What *is* in Troy alone for you, Achaean lads?

The sea – and Homer too... Love sets all things in motion.[5]
Who's one to listen to? Now Homer's voice must cease
For the orations of the clamouring black seas [6]
And pounding rumble as they come close to my cushion.

1915

* * *

Умывался ночью на дворе.
Твердь сияла грубыми звезда́ми.[7]
Звездный луч — как соль на топоре,
Стынет бочка с полными краями.

На замок закрыты ворота́,
И земля по совести сурова.
Чище правды свежего холста
Вряд ли где отыщется основа.[8]

Тает в бочке, словно соль, звезда,
И вода студеная чернее,
Чище смерть, соленее беда,
И земля правдивей и страшнее.

1921

* * *

In the yard, I take a midnight bath [9]
Under gleaming skies, a roughened star realm.
Stellar rays – salt crystals on an axe –
Shine into the chilling bathing barrel.

The back gate is fastened with a pin,
Lies the earth in righteous consternation.
Purer than the truth of canvas clean
One could hardly find a foundation.

In the barrel, stars, like salt, dissolve,
With the chilly water getting darker,
Death yet purer, loss replete with salt, [10]
And the earth in truth and horror starker.

1921

Notes

[1] Сей is an archaic, and literary, demonstrative pronoun meaning "this" (masculine). The modern Russian equivalent is этот.

[2] Витийствовать is an archaic word meaning "to orate" (from вития, orator).

[3] The long (sleep-inducing?) passage in Book 2 of the *Iliad* (2. 494–760) which lists the Achaean leaders and the number of ships commanded by them.

[4] Homer repeatedly compares warriors with flying birds, including cranes. Ornithological metaphors with respect to ships are common in the Russian poetic tradition.

[5] A possible reference to the last line of *La Commedia Divina*: "L'amor che move il sole e l'altre stelle". Note also that the earlier "I've read ... down to the middle" may in this case be seen as alluding to the famous opening passage of the same work: "Nel mezzo del cammin di nostra vita...". Incredibly, the poem was written in the year that turned out to be the middle point of Mandelstam's life.

The form of the last stanza is different from that of the previous two, with the masculine and feminine rhymes swapped: *AbbA* rather than *aBBa*.

[6] Apart from the eternal voice of the sea at night, Mandelstam means the geographic Black Sea: the poem was written in The Crimea. The Black Sea belonged to the ancient Greek world (Troy is not far from it), which enhances the connection to Homer and his characters felt by the author. There is also a possible direct reference to the *Iliad* here: sailing "over the wine-black sea" (επί οίνοπα πόντον) is mentioned in the middle of the catalogue of ships (2. 613), i.e. near the point where the author stops reading. Mandelstam, educated in the universities of St Petersburg, The Sorbonne and Heidelberg, could well have been reading Homer in the original, but it is worth noting that the expression in question, which also occurs elsewhere in the *Iliad* (7. 88) and in the *Odyssey* (3. 286), is rendered as "по черному понту" (over the black sea) in the classical Russian translation of the *Iliad* by Nikolai Gnedich (1784–1833).

[7] Звезда́ми is a poetic variant of the plural ablative of звезда (star). The normative form is звёздами.

8 The words that form the rhyme between lines 6 and 8 carry relevant secondary meanings in the context of canvas (the word at the end of line 7). Суровый generally means stern, but when applied to a fabric it qualifies it as coarse or unrefined. Основа means basis or foundation, but it is also warp of the "warp and weft" pair in textile manufacturing: the warp threads provide core support to the product and tend to be stronger and more coarse than the weft threads. Some readers see a towel there ("суровое полотенце" used to be a common expression) and some a fresh shirt, enhancing the theme of sacrifice. Either way the connotations of the rhyming words strengthen the central image of the poem: the coarse and pure fabric of life which is revealed to the poet who has matured and is prepared to deal with hardship and loss and to turn them into art. Fresh canvas can also be interpreted as artists' canvas, stretched and ready to be painted on.

9 In the original he is not taking a bath, but rather washing his face and possibly upper torso. There is no verb in English that could adequately convey not only the action of умываться, but also the ritual cleansing associated with it in Slavic cultures since pre-Christian time. The process denoted by the Russian word requires the cupped hands to be filled with a fresh portion of water every time, which is immediately used and discarded. There are several indications in the poem that Mandelstam fully intended the ritual meaning of the washing, so taking a cold bath was chosen as a substitute in English.

10 Salt is associated with sacrifice (Lev. 2: 13) and purification (2 Kings 2: 21, Ezra 16: 4) in the Old Testament and is mentioned in that context in Mark 9: 49. It is also referred to as punishment in Judg. 9: 45 and as instrument of God's wrath in Gen. 19: 26 and Deut. 29: 23.

All the key words of the poem (star/stellar, salt, chilling/chilly, barrel, earth, pure, truth) make a striking re-appearance in the last stanza, with the two most important words – "star" and "salt" – occurring three times in the poem. This feature of the original is preserved in the translation.

Expert opinion is divided on whether or not Mandelstam was already aware of the execution of his friend Nikolai Gumilyov (a poet included in this anthology) at the time of writing.

Марина Цветаева

1892—1941

* * *

Красною кистью
Рябина зажглась.
Падали листья.
Я родилась.

Спорили сотни
Колоколов.
День был субботний:
Иоанн Богослов.

Мне и доныне
Хочется грызть
Жаркой рябины
Горькую кисть.

1916

Marina Tsvetayeva

1892–1941

* * *

Orange-red bunches:
A rowan alight.
Leaf avalanches.
I started life.

Hundreds of clappers
Vied for a tone.
Saturday clangour:
The Eve of St John.[1]

I fully grown
Still wish to crunch
On a hot rowan
Bitter-ripe bunch.

1916

* * *

Хочу у зеркала, где муть
И сон туманящий,
Я выпытать — куда Вам путь
И где пристанище.

Я вижу: мачты корабля,
И Вы — на палубе...
Вы — в дыме поезда... Поля
В вечерней жалобе...

Вечерние поля в росе,
Над ними — во́роны...
— Благославляю Вас на все
Четыре стороны!

* * *

I gaze into a looking glass,[2]
Where fog is cognisant,
Divining where it leads, your path.
Where is your journey's end?

I see a ship's mast out at sea
And, firm on deck, your stance...
You in train smoke... An endless lea
In evening remonstrance...

The evening lea awash with dew
And ravens on the wing...
– Be gone! My blessings are to you
Wherever travelling!

Notes

[1] Tsvetayeva was born on Saturday, October 8. October 9 (September 21 in the Eastern Orthodox calendar) is the Repose of the Holy Apostle and Evangelist John the Theologian, the patron saint of authors. There is an Orthodox tradition to ring church bells on the eve of a fest.

It is believed that St John died a natural death – the only Apostle to do so. Tsvetayeva, along with the majority of the poets included in this chapter of the anthology, did not.

[2] The form of the original is unusual in employing dactylic rhymes in iamb: *aB'aB'*. This, and the drastic difference in metrical length (4 feet versus 2), creates a strong contrast between the odd and even lines and makes the poem really stand out rhythmically:

```
∪– ∪– ∪– ∪–
∪– ∪–∪∪
∪– ∪– ∪– ∪–
∪– ∪–∪∪
```

Владимир Маяковский

1893—1930

А ВЫ МОГЛИ БЫ?

Я сразу смазал карту будня,
плеснувши краску из стакана;
я показал на блюде студня
косые скулы океана.
На чешуе жестяной рыбы
прочел я зовы новых губ.
А вы
ноктюрн сыграть
могли бы
на флейте водосточных труб?

1913

Vladimir Mayakovsky

1893–1930

C OULD Y OU?

I smudged the map of grey existence
by splashing paint out of a tumbler;
then on a plate of jellied beef tongue
I saw an ocean's cheekbones lumber;
when tin-fish scales were at my next turn,[1]
I read on them new lips' pursuit.
And you?
Could *you*
perform a nocturne
on rain-drain downpipes' bass pan flute?

1913

БРУКЛИНСКИЙ МОСТ

Издай, Кулидж,
радостный клич!

На хорошее
            и мне не жалко слов.
От похвал
            красней,
                    как флага нашего материйка,
хоть вы
            и разъюнайтед стетс [2]
                            оф
Америка.

Как в церковь
            идет
                    помешавшийся верующий,
как в скит
            удаляется,
                    строг и прост,
так я
            в вечерней
                    сереющей мерещи [3]
вхожу,
            смиренный, на Бруклинский мост.

Как в город
            в сломанный
                            прет победитель
на пушках — жерлом
                            жирафу под рост —
так, пьяный славой,
                    так жить в аппетите,
влезаю,
            гордый,
                    на Бруклинский мост.

Как глупый художник
                    в мадонну музея

Vladimir Mayakovsky

THE BROOKLYN BRIDGE [4]

Hey, Coolidge,[5]
what a cool bridge! [6]

I, too, give credit
                 where credit is due.
From praise
             blush red
                       like our banners verily,
You,
so damn united
                states
                      of America.

As a crazed zealot
                   enters
                         a chapel,
or a cloister
              where life
                         is prayer-rich,
so I,
      in the light
                   of this city chargrilled,
humbly step
            on the Brooklyn Bridge.

As victorious troops
                     enter
                           cities defeated
on cannons – with barrels
                          giraffe-high pitched –
so I, high on glory,
                     on life joy feasting,
mount,
       proud,
              the Brooklyn Bridge.

As a painter's eye
                   a museum collection

вонзает глаз свой,

влюблен и остр,

так я,

с поднебесья,

в звезды усеян,

смотрю

на Нью-Йорк

сквозь Бруклинский мост.

Нью-Йорк

до вечера тяжек

и душен,

забыл,

что тяжко ему

и высо́ко,

и только одни

домовьи души

встают

в прозрачном свечении окон.

Здесь

еле зудит

элевейтеров зуд.

И только

по этому —

тихому зуду

поймешь —

поезда

с дребезжаньем ползут,

как будто

в буфет убирают посуду.

Когда ж,

казалось, с-под речки начатой

развозит

с фабрики

сахар лавочник, —

то

под мостом проходящие мачты

размером

не больше размеров булавочных.

devours steadily,
                    unable to switch,
so I,
      from the skies
                    among constellations,
behold
        New York
                    through the Brooklyn Bridge.

New York
          has forgotten its height
                              and deportment
in slow
        and stifling
                    sunset airflow,
and only the souls
                    of its boiling apartments
rise
      in their windows' transparent glow.

Here
      the elevateds
                    produce a thin grind;
I,
    by their barely
                    audible sound,
know
        for sure
                    a train has arrived,
jarring
        like plates being put in a sideboard.

When
        from the mill on the riverside ridge
a shopkeeper
                    fetches
                    sugar in batches,
the masts
          that are passing under the bridge
look
      no bigger in size than a matchstick.

Я горд

вот этой

стальною милей,

живьем в ней

мои видения встали —

борьба

за конструкции

вместо стилей,

расчет суровый

гаек

и стали.

Если

придет

окончание света —

планету

хаос

разделает в лоск,

и только

один останется

этот

над пылью гибели вздыбленный мост,

то,

как из косточек,

тоньше иголок,

тучнеют

в музеях стоящие

ящеры,

так

с этим мостом

столетий геолог

сумел

воссоздать бы

дни настоящие.

Он скажет:

— Вот эта

стальная лапа

соединяла

моря и прерии,

Vladimir Mayakovsky

I'm proud
          of all of this
                    steely mile
materializing
          my own
                    method:
asserting constructions,
                    denying style –
austere perfection
               in joints
                    and metal.

Should
          the world
                    soon its end reach,
chaos
          set in,
                    grinding and thrashing,
with only
          this stubbornly
                    rampant bridge
rising over the dust and the ashes,

then,
          just as bones
                    thinner than pencils
fatten
          into
                    a Tyrannosaurus Rex,
in future centuries
                    a scientist pensive
will,
          by this bridge,
                    our time
                         resurrect.

He'll say:
          "The steel
                    in this very crest
the sea and the prairies
                    once joined together;

отсюда
        Европа
                рвалась на Запад,
пустив
        по ветру
                индейские перья.

Напомнит
        машину
                ребро вот это —
сообразите,
                хватит рук ли,
чтоб, став
        стальной ногой
                    на Мангетен,
к себе
        за губу
                притягивать Бруклин?

По проводам
                электрической пряди —
я знаю —
                эпоха
                после пара —
здесь
        люди
            уже
                орали по радио,
здесь
        люди
            уже
                взлетали по аэро.[7]

Здесь
        жизнь
            была
                одним — беззаботная,
другим —
        голодный
                протяжный вой.

from here
        Europe
            was marching West,
trampling
        over
            Indian feathers.

This rib
        could not
            have been manhandled,
machines propelled it
            with blocks and pulleys
to set
        a steel foot
            on Manhattan
while Brooklyn's
        lip
            towards it pulling.

And those
        yarns of electric wires
were made
        in the post-steam-power
                era;
these
    people
        already
            used the wireless,
these
    people
        already
            flew in the aero.

Here
    life
        was –
            for some – jolly,
Others
        howled,
            hungry and wronged.

Отсюда

        безработные

в Гудзон

           кидались

                   вниз головой.

И дальше

        картина моя

                без загвоздки

по струнам-канатам,

                аж звездам к ногам.

Я вижу —

        здесь

                стоял Маяковский,

стоял

        и стихи слагал по слогам. —

Смотрю,

        как в поезд глядит эскимос,

впиваюсь,

        как в ухо впивается клещ.

Бруклинский мост —

да...

        Это вещь!

1925

From here
      the jobless
into the Hudson [8]
         jumped
            headlong.

Along
     these cables
         my eyeball is coasting
into the depth
       of the universe.
I see
    that here
       stood Mayakóvsky.
He stood
      and strung his accentual verse." [9]

I'm looking,
      like an Indian looks at a fridge,
with my eye piercing
        like a tick through skin.
The Brooklyn Bridge...
Yes,
    it's the thing!

1925

Notes

1 A hanging sign of a fishmonger's shop.

2 Разъюнайтед is an irregular word derived from the Russian transliteration of the word "united" following the morphological pattern of words such as распрекрасный. "So damn united" of the translation comes very close to the intended meaning of this artificial Russian word.

3 Мерещь is a rare example of analytical behaviour in Russian morphology, an affixless radical. This noun is derived from the verb мерещиться in its second, archaic, meaning: to be faintly visible.

4 The signature stepladder layout employed by Mayakovsky in his mature period makes this poem look longer than it actually is. While this is the longest piece in the anthology (though not by much), it still contains only 66 verse lines.

5 Calvin Coolidge (John Calvin Coolidge, Jr), the president of the United States in 1923–29.

6 Mosaic rhymes of the "Coolidge"-"cool bridge" kind are typical of Mayakovsky's style, but there is no such rhyme in the original opening lines of 'The Brooklyn Bridge' (whose literal meaning is "Coolidge, give a cry of joy!"). A famous example from another poem by Mayakovsky is "делать жизнь с кого"-"Дзержинского" where a chain of 4 words is rhymed with a whole surname. Several Russian poets of modernist persuasion experimented with serious mosaic rhymes in the beginning of the 20th century, but those attempts were ultimately unsuccessful and the first poets who made such rhymes sound completely natural were arguably Vladimir Vysotsky and Joseph Brodsky half a century later. The mosaic rhymes by Mayakovsky were usually half-serious: the pun was intended but it was not the whole point. This worked very well in his poetry.

7 "Взлетали по аэро" is an irregular expression intended to be structurally and stylistically parallel to "орали по радио" from the previous line. Аэро in this context is a truncation of the word аэроплан which, in turn, is a transliteration of "aeroplane" and was used during the early days of aviation until it was superseded by the word самолет invented by the poet Velimir Khlebnikov (1885–1922), which has persisted to this day.

Vladimir Mayakovsky

8 Mayakovsky must have mistaken the East River for the Hudson River. It is unlikely that the mistake was never pointed out to him, so he probably did not correct the name deliberately.

It is also possible that the discrepancy was intentional in the first place. This stanza is apparently missing from early manuscripts, and it feels slightly awkward in the overall logical flow of the poem. It could have been added at a later stage, but this is by no means certain.

9 The original reads "composed his verse syllable by syllable". The form of 'The Brooklyn Bridge' can be analysed either as *dolnik* with a few minor metrical flaws or as accentual verse; the stepladder layout supports the latter view. *Dolnik* is rendered in translation as disciplined accentual verse anyway: see p. xxvi. Mayakovsky was famously dismissive about such subtleties and keen on innovation (which did not prevent him from being supremely competent in using traditional metres).

Сергей Есенин

1895—1925

* * *

Отговорила роща золотая
Березовым, веселым языком,
И журавли, печально пролетая,
Уж не жалеют больше ни о ком.

Кого жалеть? Ведь каждый в мире странник —
Пройдет, зайдет и вновь покинет дом.
О всех ушедших грезит конопляник
С широким месяцем над голубым прудом.

Стою один среди равнины голой,
А журавлей относит ветром в даль,
Я полон дум о юности веселой,
Но ничего в прошедшем мне не жаль.

Не жаль мне лет, растраченных напрасно,
Не жаль души сиреневую цветь.[1]
В саду горит костер рябины красной,
Но никого не может он согреть.

Не обгорят рябиновые кисти,
От желтизны не пропадет трава,
Как дерево роняет тихо листья,
Так я роняю грустные слова.

И если время, ветром разметая,
Сгребет их все в один ненужный ком...
Скажите так... что роща золотая
Отговорила милым языком.

Sergey Yesenin

1895–1925

* * *

The golden grove is silent; it has spoken
In birch trees' animated cheery tongue.
The cranes have left, a quiet siege despondent,
Birds on their way, with all their crying done.

Who in this world to mourn when all are vagrants?
Each passes by: comes home, but soon he's gone.
Of him remain the reveries of the grain fields,
The crescent moon over the light-blue pond.

I stand alone amidst a field laid bare,
The cranes being swept away by restless winds.
I reminisce about my youth's affairs,
But of my past I do not mourn a thing.

I will not mourn years of a life being botched up,
I will not mourn soul's lilac bunch that wanes.
A rowan's flames are raging in an orchard,
But nobody Is warmed by fireless flames.

They will not singe the rowan's heavy corymbs,
The yellow grasses' roots will keep their verve.
A tree succumbs to quiet leaf outpouring,
And so will I shed off my tristful verse.

If in the end all-scattering time should gather
The lines I left into a useless heap,
Then, please, remember that I had much rather
You said: the golden grove has ceased to speak...

* * *

Слышишь — мчатся сани, слышишь — сани мчатся.
Хорошо с любимой в поле затеряться.

Ветерок веселый робок и застенчив.
По равнине голой катится бубенчик.

Эх вы, сани, сани! Конь ты мой буланый!
Где-то на поляне клен танцует пьяный.

Мы к нему подъедем, спросим — что такое?
И станцуем вместе под тальянку трое.

1925

* * *

Listen: sleighs are flying, soon they'll be arriving.
Take me with my girlfriend for a drive around!

Though the wind is merry, it is shy and fickle,
Down the empty snowfield, sleigh bells start to tinkle.

Oh my sleigh fast-sliding, oh my horse sure-footed!
There's a maple drunken, dancing in the woodland.

We will ask "how is it?" stopping as we get there,
Then to the *taliánka* we'll all dance together.[2]

1925

Notes

[1] See note 3 on p. 64. Here the related normative noun is цветение (blossom). Words of this type occur in several other poems by Yesenin.

[2] *Talianka* (тальянка) is a one-row variety of Russian harmonica, Italian in origin. Its name is a corruption of итальянка, which means Italian (noun, feminine).

A red-chested bullfinch

красногрудый снегирь

Николай Заболоцкий

1903—1958

Движение

Сидит извозчик, как на троне,
Из ваты сделана броня,
И борода, как на иконе,
Лежит, монетами звеня.
А бедный конь руками машет,
То вытянется, как налим,
То снова восемь ног сверкают
В его блестящем животе.

1927

Nikolai Zabolotsky

1903–1958

MOTION

The cabbie postures like a monarch,
his armour being a woolly quilt.
His beard, appearing old-iconic,
shows off with pennies' chinking lilt.[1]
The horse, a poor thing, is handwaving,
now he is stretched up like an eel
and now again eight legs are gleaming
in his reflective shiny paunch.[2]

1927

Можжевеловый куст

Я увидел во сне можжевеловый куст.
Я услышал вдали металлический хруст.
Аметистовых ягод услышал я звон.
И во сне, в тишине, мне понравился он.

Я почуял сквозь сон легкий запах смолы.
Отогнув невысокие эти стволы,
Я заметил во мраке древесных ветвей
Чуть живое подобье улыбки твоей.

Можжевеловый куст, можжевеловый куст,
Остывающий лепет изменчивых уст,
Легкий лепет, едва отдающий смолой,
Проколовший меня смертоносной иглой!

В золотых небесах за окошком моим
Облака проплывают одно за другим.
Облетевший мой садик безжизнен и пуст...
Да простит тебя бог, можжевеловый куст!

1957

JUNIPER SHRUB

In a dream I was seeing a juniper shrub.
Then I heard, from afar, metal crunch tensing up
And the amethyst berries produce a faint chime.
In my slumber I liked their sweet music sublime.

I could feel through my sleep a weak odour of tar.
Having bent the short stalks sideways not very far,
In the darkness inside I observed in a while
A dim, perishing vision resembling your smile.

In the juniper shrub, in the juniper shrub
Were your treacherous lips with their cooling-down throb,
A soft prattle that only just savoured of tar
And impaled me at once on the point of its spar.

Now the golden sky gleams in my room's window frame
And the clouds there are busily ferrying rain
While my orchard autumnal looks lifeless and drab...
May the good Lord forgive you, oh juniper shrub!

1957

Notes

[1] In keeping with the overall style of the book *Столбцы* (*Columns*), this line is likely to be a deliberate puzzle inviting interpretations. Some of the explanations which have been proposed are:

- The larger-than-life beard entangles with, or even continues as, the mane of the cabbie's horse (which at the time would often be decorated with coin-like pendants). This interpretation is consistent with the grotesque, multiple-viewpoint depiction of the cabbie and his horse.
- The colour of the beard is ginger, making its ringlets look similar to copper pennies to the extent that they appear to make a chinking sound.
- The sound of coins is made by the frozen strands of the cabbie's beard; it is a winter scene, as evidenced by the wool (cotton-wool in the original) armour worn by him. The comparison with an icon may be taken to support this view: beards in icons often look as if they consist of individual strands of hair.

[2] According to the memoirs of Andrey Sergeyev (1933–1998), Zabolotsky claimed that he had, for many years, believed that both quatrains of this poem were rhymed.

Nikolai Zabolotsky

Леонид Мартынов

1905—1980

Чистое небо

Не ювелирные изделия,
Не кости для пустой игры,
Не кружевные рукоделия,
И не узорные ковры,
Не шелка облако душистое,
Не цирк
И даже не кино,
А покажу вам небо чистое.
Не видывали давно?
Быть может, книгу перелистывая,
Вы скажете:
Какое мглистое,
Какое смутное оно!
Бывает так...
Но всё равно
Я покажу вам
Небо чистое.

1945, 1956

Leonid Martynov

1905–1980

Unclouded Sky

Not chains of gold with polished opal rocks
Not games with dice to kill one's time
And not hand-crafted lace in openworks
Nor patterned rugs made of thin twine,
Not perfumed silk, puffed-up and rounded,
Not entertainment –
                any style:
I'll show you all the sky unclouded.
Not seen it for a long-long while?
As you leaf through, as you begin to read,
You may proclaim:
"There's murkiness to it;
It has a rather hazy feel!"
Sometimes this happens...
But I still
Will show you all
The sky unclouded.

1945, 1956

* * *

Весна,
Как незримая птица из тех,
Которые ветрено мчатся с морей,
Когтями вцепилась во вздыбленный мех
Ушанки моей.

«Зачем же ты шапку мне рвешь с головы?
Еще холода!»
— «А разве не чувствуешь запах травы
От снега и льда?»

«Я чувствую! Боже меня сохрани
Терять этот нюх.
Закат, озаряющий вешние дни,
Еще не потух!

Еще я и нынче умею весну
За крылья хватать.
И ночью сегодня, лишь только засну,
Я буду летать.»

* * *

Springtime,
like the kind of invisible bird
that's hurtled by winds blowing inland from seas,
thrust wildly its claws in my bristling hat – furred,
and lined with warm fleece.

"Wherefore are you trying to snatch up my hat?
It's still cold at nights!"
– "You surely must smell the new grass roots, and that
Does come off the ice."

"Indeed I can smell them! This gift is a grace
I pray to retain.
The sunset of Spring has illumined her days,
But has yet to wane.

Still now, as before, I can capture that slick
Spring's pinions spry.
And later tonight, just as I fall asleep,
I'm sure I will fly."

Семен Кирсанов

1906—1972

Строки в скобках

Жил-был — я.
(Стоит ли об этом?)
Шторм бил в мол.
(Молод был и мил...)
В порт плыл флот.
(С выигрышным билетом
жил-был я.)
Помнится, что жил.

Зной, дождь, гром.
(Мокрые бульвары...)
Ночь. Свет глаз.
(Локон у плеча...)
Шли всю ночь.
(Листья обрывали...)
«Мы», «ты», «я»
нежно лепеча.

Знал соль слёз
(Пустоту постели...)
Ночь без сна
(Сердце без тепла) —
гас, как газ,
город опустелый.
(Взгляд без глаз,
окна без стекла.)

Где ж тот снег?
(Как скользили лыжи!)
Где ж тот пляж?
(С золотым песком!)

Semyon Kirsanov

1906–1972

Words and Brackets

Once. I. Was.
(Is it worth to speak of?)
Storm. Hit. Pier.
(I was young and yet...)
Fleet. Reached. Port.
(And a winning ticket...)
Once. I. Had.
(Still I can't forget.)

Heat. Rain. Flash.
(Avenues in downpours...)
Night. Eyes. Glow.
(Curls of shoulder length.)
Walk. All. Night.
(...stripping leaves from arbours.)
"You". "Me". "Us".
(...cooing under breath.)

Knew. Salt. Tears.
(A lone bed – for certain...)
Night. No. Sleep.
(Cold in one's heart reigns.)
Quenched. Like. Gas.
(...was the town deserted.)
Glance. No. Eyes.
(Absent window panes.)

Gone. That. Snow.
(On a piste. Slide over!)
Gone. That. Beach.
(Lots of golden sand!)

Где тот лес?
(С шепотом — «поближе».)
Где тот дождь?
(«Вместе, босиком!»)

Встань. Сбрось сон.
(Не смотри, не надо...)
Сон не жизнь.
(Снилось и забыл.)
Сон как мох
в древних колоннадах.
(Жил-был я...)
Вспомнилось, что жил.

Gone. That. Grove.
(Whisper: "hold me, lover!")
Gone. That. Rain.
("Let's run hand in hand!")

Wake. Shake. Dream.
(Don't you look, it's cruel.)
Dream. Not. Life.
(Seen it and forgot.)
Dream. Like. Moss.
(...over ancient ruins)
Once. I. Was.
(I recall I was.)

* * *

Эти летние дожди,
эти радуги и тучи —
мне от них как будто лучше,
будто что-то впереди.

Будто будут острова,
необычные поездки,
на цветах — росы подвески,
вечно свежая трава.

Будто будет жизнь, как та,
где давно уже я не был,
на душе, как в синем небе
после ливня — чистота...

Но опомнись — рассуди,
как непрочны, как летучи
эти радуги и тучи,
эти летние дожди.

* * *

Those midsummer rains that spread,
all those rainbows and dark clouds
seem to help my world go round,
seem to point to things ahead;

seem to promise happy isles,
lawns exuberantly verdant,
flowers trimmed with dewy pendants,
and adventures – endless miles;

promise me a world unseen,
like the one I used to wander
with my soul like the blue yonder
after rainfall squeaky clean...

Oh get real and use your head:
speedily will peter out
all those rainbows and dark clouds,
those midsummer rains that spread.

Арсений Тарковский

1907—1989

ПЕРВЫЕ СВИДАНИЯ

Свиданий наших каждое мгновенье
Мы праздновали, как богоявленье,
Одни на целом свете. Ты была
Смелей и легче птичьего крыла,
По лестнице, как головокруженье,
Через ступень сбегала и вела
Сквозь влажную сирень в свои владенья
С той стороны зеркального стекла.

Когда настала ночь, была мне милость
Дарована, алтарные врата
Отворены, и в темноте светилась
И медленно клонилась нагота,
И, просыпаясь: «Будь благословенна!» —
Я говорил и знал, что дерзновенно
Мое благословенье: ты спала,
И тронуть веки синевой вселенной
К тебе сирень тянулась со стола,
И синевою тронутые веки
Спокойны были, и рука тепла.

А в хрустале пульсировали реки,
Дымились горы, брезжили моря,
И ты держала сферу на ладони
Хрустальную, и ты спала на троне,
И — Боже правый! — ты была моя.

Ты пробудилась и преобразила
Вседневный человеческий словарь,
И речь по горло полнозвучной силой
Наполнилась, и слово *ты* раскрыло
Свой новый смысл и означало: *царь*.

Arseny Tarkovsky

Arseny Tarkovsky

1907–1989

First Trysts [1]

In our first meetings every minute's offering
Was celebrated as a new theophany,
Intended for the two of us. You seemed
Decisive more, and lighter, than a wing,
When down the flights of stairs, like vertigo
You skipped over the steps and out, to pass
Through clammy lilac trees, with me in tow,
Into your realm beyond the looking glass.

When night came on I had been granted favour.
The altar gates were opened; I could see
Your nakedness give off its lustrous fervour
Into the dark and lean there listlessly.
And when I woke, I muttered: "Blessed be...",
But knew the blessing wasn't mine to give:
You were asleep, and from the table vase
A lilac branch was stretching, flower and leaf,
To touch your eyelids up with dark blue cast
From this old Universe, and make them calm...
Your hand was warm, your eyelids still at last.

Inside the crystal glass some rivers pulsed,
Volcanoes smoked, seas heaved their shimmering brine,
And on your palm you held the crystal sphere.
Upon a throne you lay, and slumbered there,
And truly – goodness gracious! – you were mine.

And then you woke. You instantly transformed
The names that humans give to every thing
To wrest those silent names from vocal chords,
Revealing a new meaning of the word
That had the sound of *you*, but it meant *king*.

На свете всё преобразилось, даже
Простые вещи — таз, кувшин, — когда
Стояла между нами, как на страже,
Слоистая и твердая вода.

Нас повело неведомо куда.
Пред нами расступались, как мира́жи,[2]
Построенные чудом города,
Сама ложилась мята нам под ноги,
И птицам с нами было по дороге,
И рыбы поднимались по реке,
И небо развернулось пред глазами…

Когда судьба по следу шла за нами,
Как сумасшедший с бритвою в руке.

Arseny Tarkovsky

All was transfigured in the world; all, even
The jar, the sink, things simple and concrete
When once again a guard stood up between us:
A many-layered, solid water sheet.[3]

We were being led where nobody would lead.
Before us, like mirages, cities parted –
Miraculously built in lands uncharted.
Spearmints would drop their leaves under our feet,
And birds along our journey's route would flit,
And fish ascended river currents, and
The sky unfurled above the mountains, islands…[4]

When Fate was following the trail behind us,
Like a psychotic with a blade in hand.

* * *

Красный фонарик стоит на снегу.
Что-то я вспомнить его не могу.

Может быть, это листок-сирота,
Может быть, это обрывок бинта,

Может быть, это на снежную ширь
Вышел кружить красногрудый снегирь,

Может быть, это морочит меня
Дымный закат окаянного дня.

1973

* * *

I see a lantern: red on white snow,
Looking as if it's a thing that I know:

It could, perhaps, be an orphaned red leaf,
Could be a bandage – that I can believe,

Could be a red-chested bullfinch that's flown
Over wide snowfields, about to fly home,[5]

It could be even that I am beguiled
By the sundown that has spread and gone wild.[6]

1973

Notes

[1] The original is fully rhymed, but the rhymes do not follow any conventional pattern and are occasionally stretching from one free-form stanza to another, which enhances the sense of freedom conveyed by the poem. The translation takes similar liberties with the rhyme scheme.

[2] Пред is an archaic, and poetic, reduced form of the word перед (before, in front of).

The word миражи is used here with a non-normative stress on the second syllable which makes it sound old-fashioned and poetic. The normative pronunciation is миражи́.

[3] This is a second reference to a mirror in the poem. Some 10 years after writing it Tarkovsky recited 'First Trysts', and several of his other works, for the soundtrack of the cult film Зеркало (Mirror, 1974) directed by his son Andrei Tarkovsky (1932–1986).

[4] The half-reference to Rev. 6: 14, which was made more prominent in translation, sheds a different light on the whole stanza: a private, temporary reversal of the end of the world.

[5] Tarkovsky apparently associates the bullfinch with war. This bird is also mentioned, without any obvious reason, in another poem of his, written in 1942 and dealing with his combat experience directly. This may have something to do with the colour of a male bullfinch, with its dramatic appearance against the background of snow or with the way these birds suddenly arrive in middle Russia (usually with the first serious snowfall) and then disappear as they pass southwards in the course of their yearly migration. Whatever it is, the third couplet of the original, strengthened by alliteration which is reproduced in the translation, is as disturbing as the second.

See also note 3 on p. 292.

[6] It is the sundown of a cursed day in the original, which might be a reference to the memoirs Cursed Days: a Diary in Revolution by Ivan Bunin (a writer whose poems are included in this anthology). Although the adjective окаянный (cursed) is rare in modern Russian, we did not find the likelihood of this being a reference significant enough to merit special translation.

Александр Твардовский

1910—1971

МАТЕРИ

И первый шум листвы еще неполной,
И след зеленый по росе зернистой,
И одинокий стук валька на речке,
И грустный запах молодого сена,
И отголосок поздней бабьей песни,
И просто небо, голубое небо —
Мне всякий раз тебя напоминают.

Alexander Tvardovsky

1910–1971

To Mother

An early rustle of foliage that's still growing,
Green footprints over grainy dew on grasses,
The clamour of a lonely battledore,
The melancholy smell of hay being gathered,
The echo of a woman's song at sunset
And even skies, the blue, uncluttered heavens, –
Time and again, all those make me recall you.

* * *

Я знаю, никакой моей вины
В том, что другие не пришли с войны,
В том, что они — кто старше, кто моложе —
Остались там, и не о том же речь,
Что я их мог, но не сумел сберечь, —
Речь не о том, но всё же, всё же, всё же...

1966

* * *

I know I shouldn't really be contrite
About the others, who in mortal fight
Were lost. Some young, some not, they were forever
Left in that war. Though no-one ever said
That any one of them I could have saved,
I have no peace, not then, not now, not ever...

1966

Ярослав Смеляков

1913—1972

Земляки

Когда встречаются этапы
Вдоль по дороге снеговой,
Овчарки рвутся с жарким храпом
И злее бегает конвой.

Мы прямо лезем, словно танки,
Неотвратимо, будто рок.
На нас — бушлаты и ушанки,
Уже прошедшие свой срок.

И на ходу колонне встречной,
Идущей в свой тюремный дом,
Один вопрос, тот самый, вечный,
Сорвавши голос, задаем.

Он прозвучал нестройным гулом
В краю морозной синевы:
«Кто из Смоленска? Кто из Тулы?
Кто из Орла? Кто из Москвы?»

И слышим выкрик деревенский,
И ловим отклик городской,
Что есть и тульский, и смоленский,
Есть из поселка под Москвой.

Ах, вроде счастья выше нету —
Сквозь индевелые штыки
Услышать хриплые ответы,
Что есть и будут земляки.

Шагай, этап, быстрее, шибко,[1]
забыв о собственном конце,
С полублаженною улыбкой
На успокоенном лице.

1964

Yaroslav Smelyakov

1913–1972

FELLOW TOWNSMEN [2]

When prison convoys, on a byway
That's been snowed over, get to meet,
The dogs start pulling, panting, steaming,
And frenzied guards rush to and fro.

We push ahead, as if besotted,[3]
Unstoppable like human tanks.
In ear-flapped hats and woollen jackets,
Which have already served their term.

And as we pass a group returning
Under armed escort back to jail,
A question, that eternal question,
We strain our vocal chords to ask.

In chorus, incoherent, babbling
Out of a frosty haze it comes:
"Who's from Smolénsk? Who is from Túla?
Who's from Oryól? A Muscovite?"

We hear some rural accents clearly
And also catch an urban voice;
Some say they're from Smolénsk and Túla
And others from near-Moscow towns.

Ah, there is no such bliss in heaven
Like hoarse replies that fly across
The frosty bayonets, insisting
That fellow townsmen will be there.

March ye, condemned, and get a move on,
Forget your own approaching end
And keep a half-demented simper
On every newly tranquil face.

1964

* * *

Если я заболею,
к врачам обращаться не стану,
Обращаюсь к друзьям
(не сочтите, что это в бреду):
постелите мне степь,
занавесьте мне окна туманом,
в изголовье поставьте
ночную звезду.

Я ходил напролом.
Я не слыл недотрогой.
Если ранят меня в справедливых боях,
забинтуйте мне голову
горной дорогой
и укройте меня
одеялом
в осенних цветах.

Порошков или капель — не надо.
Пусть в стакане сияют лучи.
Жаркий ветер пустынь, серебро водопада —
Вот чем стоит лечить.
От морей и от гор
так и веет веками,
как посмотришь, почувствуешь:
вечно живем.

Не облатками белыми[4]
путь мой усеян, а облаками.
Не больничным от вас ухожу коридором,
а Млечным Путем.

1940

* * *

If I am taken ill,
then I won't make appointments with doctors.
I will turn to my friends
(and I've not been delirious thus far):
Make my bed from a steppe,
drape my windows with white, wreathing fog trails
and install by my headboard
a glimmering star.

I have pushed my way through,
never hid in a crowd.
If a virtuous fight sends me into a swoon,
bandage my wounded head
with a serpentine road,
cover me
with a blanket autumnal
in bloom.

Tablets, drops... These I haven't the zeal for.
Let the water glass float sun-ray reeds.
The hot wind of a desert and waterfall silver,
that is how you should treat.
Feel the spirit of time
in the seas and the mountains;
just you look, you will sense
life's perpetual stay.

Not with white-coloured capsulets is my way strewn,
it is strewn with clouds, and
I am leaving you not by a hospital corridor,
the Milky Way.

1940

Notes

[1] Шибко is a colloquial adverb meaning "quickly" in this context.

[2] The original is written in iambic tetrameter with interleaved feminine and masculine rhymes (*AbAb*), which is an established classical form in Russian poetry. Rhyme was dropped in translation to avoid any traces of light-hearted intonation (which many of the readers of contemporary English poetry automatically associate with rhymed verse), as it would be inappropriate for the subject matter of this poem.

[3] Smelyakov was imprisoned both in the 1930s and 1950s, and also spent several years as a POW in Finland in the 1940s. As he wrote in another poem, "впечатленьями жизнь не бедна" (I have plenty of things to recall).

[4] Here, облатка is an old-fashioned starch capsule containing powdered medication.

Ян Сатуновский

1913—1982

* * *

Всё реже пью, и всё меньше;
курить почти перестал;
а что касается женщин,
то здесь я чист, как кристалл.
Поговорим о кристаллах.
Бывают кристаллы — Изольды и Тристаны.
Лоллобриджиды,
Мэрилин Монро.
Кристалл дерево
и кристалл вино.
У нас в университете кристаллографию
преподавал профессор Микей,
Александр Яковлевич.
Его посадили в 37-м.
Когда его выпустили, он
нет не могу.
А вы говорите Лоллобриджида.

Yan Satunovsky

1913–1982

* * *

A drunk – less often, less willing; [1]
smoke-free – well, I am quite near;
but in the matter of women
my record is crystal clear.
Now let us turn to the crystals.
Some crystals are Iseults and Tristans.
Lollobrigidas,
Marilyn Monroe.
Crystals arboreal,
crystal Pernod.
At our university Crystallography
was taught by Professor Mikkéy,
Alexander Yákovlevich.
They took him in '37.
When he came out, he
no I can't.
So much for Lollobrigida...

* * *

Сегодня, завтра,
некогда, вчера [2]
влечет и шепчет,
как пчела,
и некуда спешить,
и некогда гадать
сегодня, завтра,
никогда, всегда.

1966

Yan Satunovsky

* * *

Today, tomorrow,
yesterday, one day
is buzzing like a bee
and beckons me away;
there is nowhere to rush,
there is no time to guess
soon, nevermore and
till the end of days.[3]

1966

Notes

[1] Only the first 10 lines of the original are rhymed. See the discussion of the form of this poem on p. xx.

[2] The word некогда is used here in its old-fashioned meaning: once, in former times. The other occurrence four lines down is in the primary meaning: there is no time.

[3] Not a single line by Satunovsky, except for his children's poems, was published in Russia in his lifetime.

To see this day

до этого дня

Александр Галич

1918—1977

Песня про майора Чистова

Я спросонья вскочил, патлат,
Я рванулся, а сон — за мной.
Мне приснилось, что я — атлант,
На плечах моих шар земной!

И болит у меня спина,
То мороз по спине, то жар,
И, с устатку пьяней пьяна,[1]
Я роняю тот самый шар.

И ударившись об Ничто,
Покатился он, как звезда,
Через млечное решето
В бесконечное Никуда...

И так странен был этот сон,
Что ни дочери, ни жене
Не сказал я о том, что он
Этой ночью приснился мне.

Я и сам отогнал ту боль,
Будто наглухо дверь забил,
И часам к десяти ноль-ноль
Я и вовсе тот сон забыл.

Но в двенадцать ноль-ноль часов
Простучал на одной ноге
На работу майор Чистов,
Что заведует буквой «Г»!

И открыл он мое досье,
И на чистом листе, педант,
Написал он, что мне во сне
Нынче снилось, что я атлант...

Alexander Galich

1918–1977

THE BALLAD OF THE LAME MAJOR [2]

Half asleep I got up, slipshod.
I shot out, and my dream with me.
I had dreamed that I was a god
With the globe spinning on my knee.[3]

And my knee was so worn, it ached.
It grew hot and began to throb.
Like a drunk, I could not sit straight.
So I dropped it, this goddamn globe.

And it bumped into Nothingness;
Off it rolled, like a falling star,
Through the holes in our Milky nest
To the infinite Somewhere Far...

And my dream was so mighty odd,
That I felt it was not alright
To tell anyone in the world
What I'd seen when asleep last night.

So I closed off and locked my pain,
As one would shut and bolt a gate,
And no later than 10 a.m.
Did my memories grow pale and fade.

But at noon, at twelve hundred, came
To his office, in charge of Gs,
An old major, upright and lame
With a crutch knocking out a jig.

And my dossier caught his sight,
A new sheet neatly trimmed and cropped.
And he wrote: in his dream last night
Galich spun on his knee the globe.

БАЛЛАДА О СТАРИКАХ И СТАРУХАХ

С КОТОРЫМИ Я ВМЕСТЕ ЖИЛ И ЛЕЧИЛСЯ
В САНАТОРИИ ОБЛАСТНОГО СОВЕТА ПРОФСОЮЗОВ
В 110 КМ. ОТ МОСКВЫ

Все завидовали мне: «Эко денег!»[4]
Был загадкой я для старцев и стариц.
Говорили про меня: «Академик».
Говорили: «Генерал-иностранец».

О, бессоницы, снотворных отрава!
Может статься, это вы виноваты,
Что привиделась мне вздорная слава
В полумраке санаторной палаты.

А недуг со мной хитрил поминутно:
То терзал, то отпускал на поруки.
И всё было мне так странно и трудно,
А труднее всего — были звуки.

Доминошники стучали в запале;
Привалившись к покарябанной пальме,
Старцы в чёсанках с галошами спали[5]
Прямо в холле, как в общественной спальне.

Я неслышно проходил: «Англичанин!»
Я козла не забивал: «Академик!»[6]
И звонки мои в Москву обличали:
«Эко денег у него, эко денег!»

И казалось мне, что вздор этот вечен,
Неподвижен, словно солнце в зените...
И когда я говорил: «Добрый вечер!»,
Отвечали старики: «Извините».

И кивали, как глухие глухому,
Улыбались не губами, а краем:
«Мы, мол, вовсе не хотим по-плохому,
Но как надо, извините, не знаем...»

Alexander Galich

The Ballad of the Elderly People[7]

WITH WHOM I SHARED A WARD IN THE SANATORIUM
OF THE REGIONAL TRADE UNION COUNCIL,
IN A PLACE 70 MILES AWAY FROM MOSCOW

Every patient envied me: "Rich as Rothschild".
Mr Mystery to elderly dears,
I heard whispers: "A designer of rockets",
And at times: "An overseas brigadier".

Oh insomnia, your pills' venom heinous
Would have been the reason, not too unlikely,
That I fancied that I was very famous,
Lying flat in murky hospital lighting.

My disease was being ever so crafty;
Now it shook me, now it left me at poise.
And I felt at times so groggy and crabby,
But the worst thing was the hospital noise.

Dominoes were being slammed with a gusto.
In the hall, as in a dorm for the public,
Some old folks in winter boots snored in blusters,
Leaning sideways on a scratched potted palm-tree.

I would pass them noiselessly: "From Alaska";
Stayed away from dominoes: "Building rockets".
And my use of the pay phone was lambasted:
"Rich as Rothschild – I'll be damned! – rich as Rothschild."

And this nonsense promised never to leave me,
Like the sun at noon stood still, hot and horrid.
And whenever I would greet them "Good evening!"
The old folks would answer back "Very sorry".

They would nod as if a mute to a deaf one
They would smile with their mouths' corners and only:
"Well, you know, we are all making the effort...
Just not certain what is proper and comely."

Я твердил им в их мохнатые уши,
В перекурах за сортирною дверью:
«Я такой же, как и вы, только хуже!»
И поддакивали старцы, не веря.

И в кино я не ходил: «Ясно, немец!»
И на танцах не бывал: «Академик!»
И в палатке я купил чай и перец:
«Эко денег у него, эко денег!»

Ну, и ладно, и не надо о славе...
Смерть подарит нам бубенчики славы!
А живем мы в этом мире послами
Не имеющей названья державы.

I repeated into their faces earthy,
With a cigarette my craving relieving:
"I am one of you, I'm only less worthy."
And the elders would say "yes", disbelieving.

I would skip the movies: "Told you, a German!"
I'd abstain from dancing, too: "Building rockets".
At the kiosk I would buy tea with lemon:
"Rich as Rothschild – I'll be damned! – rich as Rothschild."

Well, so be it, never mind the renown…
Death will grant us those brass bells of the famous.
We are envoys for this world – of the crown
Of the kingdom that's supposed to be nameless.

Notes

---

[1] "С устатку" is an idiom meaning "while tired". It has a strong tendency to occur within the expression "выпить с устатку" (to relax over a drink having completed a tiring job or a hard day's work).

"Пьяней пьяна" is an expression equivalent to "drunker than drunk".

[2] Many poems by Galich were written as song lyrics, and he had a penchant for logaoedics which work very well in songs. The metrical scheme of this piece is ∪∪– ∪∪– ∪–.

[3] In the original the author sees himself in the dream as Atlas of Greek mythology, who is holding the globe on his shoulders (which is a common misconception: Atlas is supposed to hold the sky or the celestial sphere, not the globe).

[4] Эко followed by a noun in the genitive case is an idiomatic expression meaning "so much/many of ...".

[5] Чесанки are soft boots made of combed wool, a refined variety of валенки.

[6] "Забивать козла" (to hammer in the goat, or to slaughter the goat) is an idiom meaning to play dominoes. It has its origin is in a particular domino game whose colloquial name is козел (the goat).

[7] The metre of this poem is –∪ –∪ ∪∪– –∪ –∪, with the actual word stresses tending to follow the rhythmic pattern ∪∪´∪ ∪∪´ ∪∪´∪.

Николай Глазков

1919—1979

Ворон

Черный ворон, черный дьявол,
Мистицизму научась,
Прилетел на белый мрамор
В час полночный, черный час.

Я спросил его: «Удастся
Мне в ближайшие года
Где-нибудь найти богатство?»
Он ответил: «Никогда!»

Я сказал: «В богатстве мнимом
Сгинет лет моих орда.
Всё же буду я любимым?»
Он ответил: «Никогда!»

Я сказал: «Пусть в личной жизни
Неудачник я всегда.
Но народы в коммунизме
Сыщут счастье?» — «Никогда!»

И на все мои вопросы,
Где возможны «нет» и «да»,
Отвечал вещатель грозный
Безутешным «Никогда!»

Я спросил: «Какие в Чили
Существуют города?»
Он ответил: «Никогда!» —
И его разоблачили.

1938

Nikolai Glazkov

1919–1979

THE RAVEN

Once the Raven, inky devil,
Having learned a mystic rite,
Swooped upon the pallid bevel
Of a marble slab at night.

And I asked, "Pray tell – 'tis torture
Wond'ring what life has in store –
Will I find one day my fortune?"
Quoth the Raven, "Nevermore".

So I said, "Gold has no meaning,
'Tis but dust which fools adore.
Will I then be loved by women?"
Quoth the Raven, "Nevermore".

"Let my private life abysmal
Stay that way: I'm quite a bore…
Still, will under communism all
Men be happy?" – "Nevermore".

And to every single question
(Which would "yes" or "no" implore)
The reply the bird did fashion
Was the sullen "Nevermore"!

So I asked, "What causes gout,
Makes big toes inflamed and sore?" [1]
Quoth the Raven, "Nevermore" –
And was instantly found out. [2]

1938

* * *

Я на мир взираю из-под столика:
Век двадцатый — век необычайный, —
Чем столетье интересней для историка,
Тем для современника печальней.

* * *

Seen from under tables in Astoria,[3]
I must say the twentieth century's exciting.
What will make an age engaging to historians
Causes the contemporaries' sadness.

Notes

[1] The question in the original is "What cities are there in Chile?"

[2] This is a light-hearted reference to a deadly serious matter. The poem was written at a time when the authorities were obsessed with unmasking hidden enemies and the atmosphere in the country was bordering on hysterical. There is also an element of black humour involved here: "чёрный ворон" (black raven) was a nickname for the prisoner-transporting vehicle used by NKVD.

The switch from *AbAb* to *AbbA* rhyming in the final stanza is a feature of the original; it emphasises the trick nature of the last question.

[3] In the original it is a table in an unspecified place, but the word used there for "table" (столик rather than стол) implies a restaurant or a café. That word also forms a comical rhyme with историк (historian).

This quatrain was published both as the penultimate stanza of a longer piece 'Стихи, написанные под столом' (Verses from Under a Table) and as an untitled standalone poem; it was widely known in the latter form.

Борис Слуцкий

1919—1986

ПРОЩАНИЕ

Добро и Зло сидят за столом.
Добро уходит, и Зло встает.
(Мне кажется, я получил талон
На яблоко, что познанье дает.)

Добро надевает мятый картуз.
Фуражка форменная на Зле.
(Мне кажется — с плеч моих сняли груз
И нет неясности на всей земле.)

Я слышу, как громко глаголет Зло: [1]
— На этот раз тебе повезло. —
И руку протягивает Добру
И слышит в ответ: — Не беру.

Зло не разжимает сведенных губ.
Добро разевает дырявый рот,
Где сломанный зуб и выбитый зуб,
Руина зубов встает.

Оно разевает рот и потом
Улыбается этим ртом.
И счастье охватывает меня:
Я до́жил до этого дня.

1954

Boris Slutsky

1919–1986

PARTING [2]

Good and Evil: a desk depth apart.
Good is leaving, and Evil must rise.
(It feels like I've got the ration card
To buy one apple of knowledge, ripe.)

Good is dressed in a tatty old vest.
Evil adjusts its pressed uniform.[3]
(I feel a load drops off my chest,
And nothing is vague anymore.)

I hear Evil pontificate:
"This time lucky, next time – watch."
It offers Good its hand for a shake
Back comes the reply, "I won't".

Evil stiffens its sealed-up lips.
Good opens up the hole in its mouth,
With one tooth missing, another split,
A ruin of teeth pokes out.

It opens up its gaping hole
With a smile, nothing left to say.
And joy is overwhelming my soul:
I have lived to see this day.

1954

* * *

Когда мы вернулись с войны,
я понял, что мы не нужны.
Захлебываясь от ностальгии,
от несовершённой вины,
я понял: иные, другие,
совсем не такие нужны.

Господствовала прямота,
и вскользь сообщалося людям,[4]
что заняты ваши места
и освобождать их не будем,

а звания ваши, и чин,
и все ордена, и медали,
конечно, за дело вам дали.
Всё это касалось мужчин.

Но в мир не допущен мужской,
к обужам его и одёжам,[5]
я слабою женской рукой
обласкан был и обнадежен.

Я вдруг ощущал на себе
то черный, то синий, то серый,
смотревший с надеждой и верой
взор. И перемену судьбе

пророчествовали и гласили
не опыт мой и не закон,
а взгляд,
и один только он —
то карий, то серый, то синий.

Они поднимали с земли,
они к небесам увлекали,
и выжить они помогли —
то синий, то серый, то карий.

Boris Slutsky

* * *

...But when we returned from the war,
I learned: we were wanted no more.
While choking on my recollections
and guilt with no rational core,
I learned we were in for rejection,
our kind not the men being looked for.

Forthrightness the call of the day,
returnees were given a "sorry":
your place has been taken away,
you're out, this is it, end of story;

and as for your rank, then again,
your medals of honour and orders
were properly earned and awarded.
That was what we'd hear from men.

Deprived of a pass to men's world,
its labour, rewards and contentions,
I was so much heartened and warmed
by women's continual attention.

I suddenly felt on my face
a green or a black or a hazel,
uplifting, elating and faithful,
gaze; and a new turn of fate

came then prophesied and pronounced,
by – neither my knowledge, nor laws –
a glance,
which was all that there was:
blue-green, hazel, amber or brown.

The glances would help me to fly
from earth all the way to the heavens,
and thanks to them all, I survived:
to blue ones, to green ones, to grey ones.

Notes

[1] Глаголать is an archaic, and Church Slavonic, verb meaning to speak or to narrate. This word can be used poetically in modern Russian. It is derived from the word глагол which now means "verb" but whose original meaning was "speech".

[2] The metre of the original is a *dolnik*: generally 4 beats, but with 3-beat final lines in the last three stanzas (in the translation – in the last 4 stanzas).

The rhyme scheme is *abab* in stanzas 1, 2 and 4 and *aabb* in stanzas 3 and 5. All the rhymes are masculine, so the variation of the rhyming scheme has only a moderate effect on intonation and does not appear to be an important feature of the poem. The translation sticks to the *abab* scheme throughout.

[3] In the original it is a wrinkled civilian peak cap vs. a service cap.

[4] Сообщалося is a colloquial form of сообщалось (here meaning "was communicated").

[5] Одёжа is a colloquial variant of the word одежда (clothes). Обужа is an artificial word made up by Slutsky for ironic effect. It was derived from обувь (footwear) following the same morphological pattern as in одёжа.

Boris Slutsky

Игорь Холин

1920—1999

* * *

Вы слышите звуки
Разлуки
Холин
Кончается
Впрочем
Кто его знает
Всякое с ним бывает
Может он не кончается
Может он
Оживает

Igor Kholin

1920–1999

* * *

Do you hear them
Wail
Khólin
Is passing away
Although
With this poet
nothing's a safe bet
Maybe he is not passing away
But rising
From the dead

РЕКА

У реки,
У реки
Голубели
Кусты,
По реке,
По реке
Проплывали
Плоты,
И сновали
Суда
И туда,
И сюда.
А за ними
Баржа́,
Еле-еле
Дыша.
Убегала
Река
За леса,
За леса,
Утекала
Река
В небеса.
В небеса.

Igor Kholin

The Stream [1]

By the stream,
By the stream
Shrubs were being
So blue.
Down the stream,
Down the stream
Rafts were leaving
The view.
Boats were heaving
Away
Both this way
And that way.
One was tugging
A barge
Which was slow
And large.
And the stream ran
Around
Woody isles,
Woody isles.
And the stream ran
To ground
In the skies.
In the skies.

Notes

¹ The original of this poem, written for children, imitates the meandering of a stream by its ever-changing rhyme pattern (*aaXb ccDb Deee XfXf Ghii Ghii*) and by shifting the rhythmic organisation after the first 8 lines. The translation meticulously reproduces these features.

Igor Kholin

That intense blue colour

синего-синего

Давид Самойлов

1920—1990

Сороковые...

Сороковые, роковые,
Военные и фронтовые,
Где извещенья похоронные
И перестуки эшелонные.

Поют накатанные рельсы.
Просторно. Холодно. Высóко.
И погорельцы, погорельцы
Кочуют с запада к востоку...

А это я на полустанке
В своей замурзанной ушанке,
Где звездочка не уставная,
А вырезанная из банки.

Да, это я на белом свете,
Худой, веселый и задорный.
И у меня табак в кисете,
И у меня мундштук наборный.[1]

И я с девчонкой балагурю,
И больше нужного хромаю,
И пайку надвое ломаю,
И всё на свете понимаю.

Как это было! Как совпало —
Война, беда, мечта и юность!
И это всё в меня запало
И лишь потом во мне очнулось!..

Сороковые, роковые,
Свинцовые, пороховые...
Война гуляет по России,
А мы такие молодые!

1961

David Samoilov

David Samoilov

1920–1990

THE FORTIES

The forties, oh those fateful forties: [2]
Armed forces and their front-line sorties,
With KIA notifications
And troop trains' calling at the stations.

The rails' habitual staccato,
The view that's spacious, cold and lofty;
And people from their places cut off,
By the West-East commotion locked in.

And here I stand upon a platform,
Dirt on my scruffy tied-up flapped cap
On which the red star is non-standard,
Cut out from a discarded flat can.

Yes, that is me in this world standing:
Thin, boisterous, full of life and happy.[3]
My pouch has some tobacco stashed in.
My cig'rette-holder nicely lacquered.

And I am chatting with a girlie,
And limping more than I would need to,
And break a piece of rye bread in two,
And think I understand all things, too.

They happened and they coincided:
The war, disasters, youth and daydreams;
And all of them got stuck inside me,
And only later did the bell ring.

The forties, oh those fateful forties,
Lead laden and gun-powder courting...
The war's the world's, the war is Russian;
And we, the youth, are there in action!

1961

ДУЭТ ДЛЯ СКРИПКИ И АЛЬТА

М.П.

Моцарт в легком опьяненье [4]
Шел домой.
Было дивное волненье,
День шальной.

И глядел веселым оком
На людей
Композитор Моцарт Вольфганг
Амадей.

Вкруг него был листьев липы
Легкий звон.
«Тара-тара, тили-тики, —
Думал он. —

Да! Компания, напитки,
Суета.
Но зато дуэт для скрипки
И альта».

Пусть берут его искусство
Задарма. [5]
Сколько требуется чувства
И ума!

Композитор Моцарт Вольфганг,
Он горазд, —
Сколько требуется, столько
И отдаст...

Ох, и будет Амадею
Дома влёт. [6]
И на целую неделю —
Черный лед.

Ни словечка, ни улыбки.
Немота.
Но зато дуэт для скрипки
И альта.

YET THERE'S THAT DUET...

M.P. [7]

Mozart's walking, somewhat tipsy
And homebound.
Life has been exciting, glitzy
All day round.

He is smiling at some bozos
On his way,
Mr Mozart, the composer,
Wolfgang A.

On a lime tree leaves are ringing,
Ding-ding-dong.
"Tarrah-tarrah, tilly-tickey",
He thinks on.

"Yes, drinks, company, free-floating
party din.
Yet there's that duet for flute and
Violin." [8]

He will give his art for nothing –
At no gain.
It requires so much passion,
So much brain!

Wolfgang Mozart the composer
Has the skill.
He'll do all it takes, no bother;
Yes, he will.

Oh you'll get domestic trouble,
Wolfgang A.
Nothing for a week but struggle,
Yea, oh yea.

Not a word will be saluting
When you're in...
Yet there's that duet for flute and
Violin.

Да! Расплачиваться надо
На миру
За веселье и отраду
На пиру,

За вино и за ошибки —
Дочиста́!
Но зато дуэт для скрипки
И альта!

Yes, new bills are on the ledger
Every day.
For the merriment and leisure
One must pay.

For the wine and motions flippant,
Errors grim...
Yet there's that duet for flute and
Violin!

Notes

[1] Here, наборный means assembled from many pieces in a mosaic pattern.

[2] The original exploits the amazing fact that the word роковые (the plural form of "fateful") is contained within the word сороковые (the forties). This work became one of the most famous post-war Russian poems, not least because of its two-word opening line which instantly imprints itself in the memory of a native speaker.

[3] The word "thin", in the sense of being malnourished, continues the chain of downbeat details revealed while zooming in from the initial all-encompassing view (which stretches with the rails beyond the horizon to the east and the west and also upwards into the strato-spheric cold) all the way down to the crude star on the dirty flapped cap. But this same word, "thin", in the sense of being youthfully slim, also forms part of the chain of upbeat details associated with the "I am doing just fine" theme. That theme starts in the previous stanza, with the red star which indicates that the narrator is a soldier rather than one of the refugees or a passive observer. So both the star and being thin belong to the downbeat and upbeat sequences at the same time: the two themes interlock in lines 11–14, forming the emotional focus of the poem. This is mirrored by the collision stated in lines 21–22, this time from a distance of many years.

[4] The normative spelling of the prepositional case of this word is опьяненьи.

[5] A colloquial modification of the adverb задаром which, in turn, is an informal variant of даром (for nothing, free of charge).

[6] A reference to the idiomatic expression "ему влетит" (he will be in trouble).

[7] According to the textologist Victor Tumarkin, the poem is dedicated to Masha Panteleeva (1956–1989), the daughter of the writer Leonid Panteleev (1908–1988).

[8] It is a duet for violin and viola in the original: see the discussion on p. xlv. There is no duet for flute and violin in Mozart's corpus, so the translation introduces a piece which he could have written, and hence makes the whole situation putative, while the original refers to an actual work by Mozart.

David Samoilov

Alexander Davydov, the author's son and one of the copyright holders, who is also an acclaimed translator of French poetry into Russian, strongly disagrees with such substitution. We are grateful to Mr Davydov for giving us the permission to publish this translation despite the disagreement.

Александр Межиров

1923—2009

* * *

Со школьной, так сказать, скамьи,
Из, в общем, неплохой семьи
Я легкомысленно попал
В гостиничный полуподвал.
Там по сукну катился шар,
И всё удар один решал,
Маркёр «Герцеговину Флор» [1]
Курил и счет провозглашал.
Перед войной, передо мной,
Величественен и суров,
В перчатке белой, нитяно́й [2]
Для протирания шаров.
Бомбоубежищем не стал
Гостиничный полуподвал.
Но в зале сделалось темно,
И на зеленое сукно,
На аспид фре́йберовских плит [3]
Какой-то черный снег летит.

1995

Alexander Mezhirov

1923–2009

* * *

Just parted with a high-school tome,
Out of a rather decent home
I stepped, without the sense of doom,
Into a semi-basement room.
A ball there rolled across the cloth,[4]
And in one shot a game was lost;
On a Herzegovína Flor[5]
Would puff the score-declaring host.
Before the war, before my face
Stern and majestic above all,
Decked with a white thread glove all days
Which one must wear to clean a ball.
Though it escaped bomb-shelter gloom,
That semi-basement of a room,
Still now the darkness has come forth,
And on the green of billiard cloth,
The smooth of perfect Freiber slates[6]
Falls snow – in hovering black flakes.

1995

* * *

Срок на зи́му военную
      в этих пределах не скуп,
Но фронты́
      по весне
          разминают затекшее тело.
Озимь плотность уже набирает,[7]
          а дуб
Всё еще в прошлогодней листве заржавелой.

Пленнный немец
      в прохладной деревне.
         Очки на носу.
         Либерал.
Никого не насиловал
      и совершенно не крал.
Не особенно миловал,
      но и не слишком карал.

Дело в бабьем кругу
      не дойдет, очевидно, до крови.
То ли ропот какой-то,
      а может быть, молитвословье.[8]

Немец пятится медленно,
      а на него тяжело
Надвигаются женщины,
      сбитые в стаю.
Он твердит: «Ничего, ничего, ничего.
Бейте, бабы, меня».
         Но слова только я понимаю.

Alexander Mezhirov

* * *

In these parts,
       war is not at all stingy with winter respite,[9]
But in spring
    the front lines
        move to stretch their extremities spastic.
Winter wheat daily strives upward into the light,
Yet an oak
    is still dressed in old foliage rusty.

Rural numbness.
      A German –
          caught up in retreat –
             a bespectacled man.
Must be liberal:
      he never pillaged, nor raped anyone.
Not a merciful angel,
      but not too much wrong has he done.

He's confronted by women.
      It looks like it won't come to slaying.
There's a grumble of sorts,
      or perhaps prayer-saying.

Now the German is backing up sluggishly
                out of their way.
Heavy footed,
    the tightly bunched womenfolk keep drawing near.
He is pleading repeatedly: "Ladies, it is quite OK.
Do it, hit me."
      And no-one but me understands what we hear.[10]

Notes

¹ Маркёр is an employee of a billiard club who is responsible for the equipment, giving instruction to the customers etc. He does not have to be a formally qualified referee.

² The normative stress in the old-fashioned adjective нитяной ("cotton" or "fabric", prepositional singular feminine) is on the first syllable.

³ Аспид in this context is slate of greyish black colour.

⁴ The game is Russian Pyramid, played with larger and heavier balls than those used in snooker or pool, on a large table with narrow, unforgiving pockets. Mezhirov had a passion for billiards and was a formidable player.

⁵ A brand of *papirósas*: cheap, strong cigarettes of large diameter, with a characteristic integrated cardboard mouthpiece and no filter. Technically, *papirosas* are not true cigarettes because the strands of tobacco in them are very short and randomly orientated. Herzegovina Flor *papirosas* were fashionable at the time, in part because Stalin favoured them (although he actually took the tobacco out and stuffed his pipe with it).

⁶ The base plates of high-quality billiard tables are made of polished slate. Billiard tables by Freiber were highly sought after, and some of them still exist. The exposed slates are part of the image of devastation, of the demise of billiard clubs in Moscow, but also a sign of the passage of time more generally.

⁷ Озимь means the shoots of winter crops.

⁸ Молитвословье is a rare word meaning the words of a prayer or the action of uttering the words of a prayer.

⁹ The metre of the original is anapaest with an intermittent additional stress on the first syllable of the line. Most lines are 5 feet long, but some are shorter or longer by one foot.

¹⁰ This line has a double meaning. His understanding the German language sets the narrator apart from the crowd but also becomes a metaphor of the incisive vision of a poet: he alone is able to perceive the situation in all its cosmic-scale (see the opening lines) grotesqueness and pathos. The gradual zooming in, all the way to the spectacles,

Alexander Mezhirov

is reminiscent of the canonical 'The Forties' by David Samoilov (p. 139), but in Mezhirov's poem the bell rings there and then rather than many years later.

Булат Окуджава

1924—1997

Синька

В южном прифронто́вом городе на рынке
торговали цыганки развесной синькой.
Торговали цыганки, нараспев голосили:
«Синяя синька! Ли́ля-лиля!»

С прибаутками торговали цыганки
на пустом рынке, в рядах пустых.
А черные мужья крутили цыгарки,
и пальцы шевелились в бородах густых.

А жители от смерти щели копали.
Синьку веселую они не покупали.
Было вдоволь у них синевы под глазами,
синего мрака погребов наказанья,
синего инея по утрам на подушках,
синей золы в печурках потухших.

И всё же не хватало синего-синего,
как матери — сына, как каравая сытного.
А синька была цвета синего неба,
которого давно у них не было, не было.

И потому, наверное, на пустом рынке,
пестрые юбки по ветру кружа,
торговали цыганки (чудеса!) синькой.
Довоенной роскошью. Без барыша.

Bulat Okudzhava

1924–1997

The Bluing

In a south, near-front-line town at market
gypsy women touted bluing by the packet.
The gypsies touted, while singing loud:
"Bluest bluing! Lalu-lalu!"

The gypsies touted with jokes and frolics
in an empty market, a deserted pitch.
The dark-skinned husbands were making rollups;
in their bushy beards did their fingers twitch.

The residents dug shelters, hoping for survival,
so the jolly bluing didn't seem of value.
They'd enough blueness under eyes puffy,
plenty of blue darkness in cellars stuffy,
blue frost on pillows in the morning hours,
blue ashes in fires that had long burnt out.

And yet they missed it, that intense blue colour –
like a mother a son, like good bread on one's palate –
while the bluing was the hue of clear blue heavens,
the kind of heavens it was clear they hadn't.

And that seemed why in an empty market,
twirling their garish skirts and petticoats,
gypsies were touting (wonder!) bluing packets.
A pre-war luxury. For sale at cost.

* * *

В земные страсти вовлеченный,
я знаю, что из тьмы на свет
однажды выйдет ангел черный
и крикнет, что спасенья нет.

Но простодушный и несмелый,
прекрасный, как благая весть,
идущий следом ангел белый
прошепчет, что надежда есть.

Bulat Okudzhava

* * *

In ways of earthly passions errant,
I know: from darkness out to light
one day will step a black-winged seraph.
"There's no salvation!" he will cry.

But, simple-minded and undaring,
delightful as the Lord's good news,
arriving next, a white-winged seraph
will whisper: "There is hope for you."

Наум Коржавин

р. 1925

* * *

> Я с детства не любил овал,
> Я с детства угол рисовал!
>
> П. Коган

Меня, как видно, Бог не звал
И вкусом не снабдил утóнченным.[1]
Я с детства полюбил овал,
За то, что он такой законченный.
Я рос и слушал сказки мамы
И ничего не рисовал,
Когда вставал ко мне углами
Мир, не похожий на овал.
Но все углы, и все печали,
И всех противоречий вал
Я тем больнее ощущаю,
Что с детства полюбил овал.

Naum Korzhavin

b.1925

* * *

> I've spurned, from childhood, the ellipse,
> My drawings angular, in flicks!
>
> P. Kogan [2]

I am not one of God's elite,
Nor am I blessed with taste or subtleness.
I've liked, from childhood, the ellipse
Because it's closed and full of suppleness.
I grew, with mummy's stories, angstless,
And I drew nothing in the least
Confronted by – with all its angles –
The world's real shape: not an ellipse.
Yet all those polygons and treasons,
All contradictions still release
More pain in me; and here's the reason:
I've liked, from childhood, the ellipse.

* * *

В наши трудные времена
Человеку нужна жена,
Нерушимый уютный дом,
Чтоб от грязи укрыться в нем.
Прочный труд и зеленый сад,
И детей доверчивый взгляд,
Вера робкая в их пути
И душа, чтоб в нее уйти.

В наши подлые времена
Человеку совесть нужна,
Мысли те, что в делах ни к чему,
Друг, чтоб их доверять ему.
Чтоб в неделю хоть час один
Быть свободным и молодым.
Солнце, воздух, вода, еда —
Всё, что нужно всем и всегда.

И тогда уже может он
Дожидаться иных времен.

1956

* * *

In our difficult, testing time
Each man needs a wife fair and fine,
And a warm and robust abode
That could shelter them both from dirt.
A good job and a garden green,
From his children a happy grin,
Cautious confidence in their course
And a soul which could him ensconce.

In our difficult bastard time
Each man should have a conscience primed,
Thoughts that earn him no wage or fees,
And a good friend to trust them with.
So that he, at least once a month,
May be free and a younger man.
Water, sunlight, fresh air and food,
As required by all for good.

Then he can be content and calm –
Waiting for different times to come.

1956

Notes

¹ The non-normative stress on the second syllable of утонченным accentuates the ironic intonation. The standard pronunciation of this word is утончённым.

² Pavel Kogan (1918–1942), a promising poet who was killed in World War II.

Константин Ваншенкин

р. 1925

ФУТБОЛИСТ

Бесконечная усталость.
Пот, катящийся с виска.
Мало времени осталось
До финального свистка.

Был я молод, бегал вволю,
Так и шастал, как челнок,
По размеченному полю,
Не жалея сильных ног.

А встречали! — как министра.
Уважительно до слез.
Операцию мениска
Я еще не перенес.

Тренированное тело
Тоже к сроку устает.
Пусть всё это пролетело,
Но во мне оно поет.

Вот судейская сирена
У судьи уже во рту.
Лужниковская арена
Оступает в темноту.

Может быть, не всем заметны
В тишине, на склоне дня,
Но отдельные моменты
Были в жизни у меня.

Бесконечная усталость,
Пот, катящийся с виска...
Мало времени осталось
До финального свистка.

Konstantin Vanshenkin

b.1925

FOOTBALLER

Tired, infinitely tired...
Perspiration in a flow.
Playing time all but expired –
To the final whistle's blow.

I was young, I ran around,
Wing to wing and goal to goal;
Zoomed across a football ground,
Chasing, strong, the leather ball.

Crowds, their rapturous ovations,
Acclamations made me cry.
The meniscus operation
Doctors hadn't yet prescribed.

Even if well-trained, a body
Must fatigue when it is time.
Everything is gone, yet oddly
Still its bells inside me chime.

I can see the referee now
Put the whistle to his lips,
And the Luzhnikí Arena [1]
Back into the darkness slips.

Though perhaps not all may comment
In the quiet of the dusk,
I would say a few fine moments
In my life did come to pass.

Tired, infinitely tired.
Perspiration in a flow...
Playing time – all but expired –
To the final whistle blow. [2]

УКЛАДКА ПАРАШЮТА

Тогда для десанта
Еще не придумали, нет,
Такого дизайна,
Как нынче: тельняшка, берет.
Одна лишь новинка
Была, отличавшая нас:
Отличная финка,
Способная радовать глаз.
Но вот ты пощупал, —
И твердой осталась рука, —
Перкалевый купол,
Густые его вороха́.
Косишься украдкой
На небо, где дыма следы,
И занят укладкой
Своей неизбежной судьбы.

2000

PACKING THE PARACHUTE

Back then, paratroopers
Wore uniforms just like the rest,
Equipped by recruiters
With neither the vests nor berets.[3]
What could get us bragging[4]
Was something no other corps had:
The slim Finnish dagger,
A pleasure to see for a lad.
Percale double-threaded,
The canopy's plentiful heap.
You feel it (lies steadied,
And firm on it, each fingertip).
A furtive glance upwind –
Smoke splotches the sky perforate –
And get busy stuffing
Your own inescapable fate.

2000

Notes

[1] The Grand Arena of the Luzhniki (Лужники) sports complex in Moscow. It is the biggest stadium in Russia (with a capacity of over 100,000 seats at the time when the poem was written), which is used mainly for football.

[2] The poem was originally published without the repeat of the first stanza, but Vanshenkin did repeat it, with a different intonation, when he recited this piece for a TV documentary in the late 1980s.

[3] The distinctive cotton vest with horizontal stripes, meant to be visible at the collar opening, has its origins in the navy but is also worn by Russian paratroopers and marines.

[4] Vanshenkin fought in World War II (and was still a teenager when it ended).

Rays empyrean

свет небесный

Инна Лиснянская

р. 1928

* * *

В овраг мы спускались, как будто в провал,
Снегами почти голубыми,
Ты палкой ореховой крупно писал
Вдоль снежной тропы мое имя.

И был набалдашник — головка змеи
И полураскрытое жало,
Я в замшевых варежках пальцы свои
От смутного страха сжимала.

Тогда бы и надо с твоей колеи
Свернуть на тропинку любую
И издали помнить улыбку змеи
И зиму почти голубую.

Inna Lisnyanskaya

b.1928

* * *

We went down a gorge which was endless and steep.
It lay dressed in white tinged with azure.
You scribbled my name with a walnut-wood stick
Alongside the snow-covered passage.

The handle was shaped like the head of a snake,
The sting half-exposed, it'd appear.
My fingers clenched up inside my mittens suede
From some inexplicable fear.

I should have left then, when a turn I could take
To veer off your trail to another,
Recall from a distance the smile of the snake,
The winter that was almost azure.

Ночи Кабирии

У всякой вещи есть предки. Так, например,
Пропеллер — потомок мельницы ветряной.
Пора дон-кихотства прошла. Бродский размер
Как уцененною куклой, играет мной, —
К чему вентилятор, когда есть кондиционер?

Но вентилятор, как видите, тоже звено
Меж веером, мельницей и самолетным винтом,
Крутящим ночи Кабирии. В этом кино
Судьба смеется глазами и плачет ртом,
Поскольку в итоге всегда не то, что дано.

Какая ирония жизни да и пера
Куклой из гуттаперчи себя наречь.
А вентиляторов предки — китайские веера
Веют с Востока и завивают смерч
Ассоциаций, которые стоят свеч.

Свечи подкорки вечного стойче огня.
Бродский, Феллини, Сервантес — обратный ход
Времени. Так доберусь до приводного ремня,
Но всуе нельзя... Пусть плачут глаза и смеется рот —
За маску сойдет гуттаперчевая броня.

Nights of Cabiria

All things have progenitors. So, indeed,
does the propeller, an heir of the sails of a mill.
The age of Quixote is over. Brodsky's beat
plays with me, as with a cheap doll, at will:
why a desk fan, when the AC best meets the need?

But, you see, the desk fan is there to link
the hand fan, the mill, and the propeller that flies,
which turns the nights of Cabiria. In that film
Fate laughs with her eyes but her mouth cries,
since one always gets what wasn't the deal.

What an irony – of life, and of my hand –
branding myself a gutta-percha doll!
The desk fan progenitors, Chinese fans
blow from the east, causing a whirl,
associations that *are* their candles' worth.

Flames of the mind, like eternal flames, are robust.
Brodsky, Fellini, Cervantes: the reverse drive
of time. I could get to the drive belt fast,
but shan't take in vain... May the mouth laugh and the eyes cry:
gutta-percha armour will do as a mask.

Глеб Горбовский

р. 1931

* * *

Когда качаются фонарики ночные[1]
И темной улицей опасно вам ходить,
Я из пивной иду, я никого не жду,
Я никого уже не в силах полюбить.

Мне дева ноги целовала, как шальная,
Одна вдова со мной пропи́ла отчий дом.
А мой нахальный смех всегда имел успех,
А моя юность — пролетела кувырком.

Лежу на нарах, как король на именинах,
И па́йку серого мечтаю получить.
Гляжу, как кот в окно, теперь мне все равно,
Я раньше всех готов свой факел потушить.

Когда качаются фонарики ночные
И черный кот бежит по улице, как черт,
Я из пивной иду, я никого не жду,
Я навсегда побил свой жизненный рекорд!

1953

Gleb Gorbovsky

b.1931

* * *

When evening gusts are swirling lamps on posts around,
To you the town's a trap 'cos thugs are on the prowl.
I leave the bar for home, I always walk alone,
I'll never be in love with nobody at all.

A virgin kissed my naked feet in wicked frenzy,
For me a widow mortgaged out her parents' place.
Oh how my brazen laughs were always praised for class!
As for my youth – it's tumbled past without a trace.

I celebrate my prison bed like kings their birthdays,
A rye-bread ration is my next most pressing goal.
I, like a cat, peek out, I am no longer proud,
I'm quite prepared to quench my torch ahead of all.

When evening gusts are swirling lamps on posts around,
A tar-black cat runs down the street, a ghost from hell.
I leave the bar for home, I always walk alone,
My own life record smashed for good by me as well!

1953

МЫЛЬНЫЕ ПУЗЫРИ

Ничего не изменилось
ни снаружи, ни внутри, —
настрогал в тарелку мыла
и пускаю пузыри.

О кровавых войнах помню,
ощущаю мысли жар;
утонченно, как японец,
созерцаю мыльный шар.

Оболочки переливы —
побежалость, перламутр...[2]
Буду весел миг счастливый
и еще полмига — мудр.

Шарик лопнул. Сохнет мыло.
Тает в пямяти узор.
Но, позвольте, что-то было!
Что-то нам ласкало взор.

...В облаках дорожной пыли,
друг мой, ангел ветровой,
мы с тобою тоже были!
Отдавали синевой![3]

Вознесенные над бездной
в оболочке продувной —
отражали свет небесный,
излучали свет земной...

1986

Gleb Gorbovsky

SOAP BUBBLES

Nothing changed – well, not a lot has,
nor within me, nor without.
I've shaved soap into hot water,[4]
and am blowing bubbles out.

I recall the time of battling,[5]
thoughts are coming in a squall;
like a Japanese, I subtly
contemplate a soapy ball.

Moving streaks, an isthmus stripy,
shifting colours, pearly eyes...
For a moment I'll be happy;
then, for half a moment, wise.

Now the bubble's burst, the pattern
starts to melt out of my mind.
I daresay still something happened,
something did caress our sight!

...In the clouds of road-dust scattered,
my good friend, my angel-wind,
you and I, we also happened!
With a modest bluish tint!

Over an abyss careering,
packed into a wind-blown case,
we reflected rays empyrean,
we emitted earthly rays...

1986

Notes

1 The original of this poem, which exists in many versions, is reproduced from an authoritative source: Горбовский Глеб. Остывшие следы. Записки литература. Лениздат, 1991, стр. 195.

2 Побежалость is a technical term: a rainbow pattern formed by a thin layer of oxidation on a metallic surface.

3 When followed by an object in the ablative case, the verb отдавать means "to give off the taste/smell/colour of ..." or "to be suggestive of ...".

4 At the time of Gorbovsky's childhood, and for a long time afterwards, children made soapy water for blowing bubbles by dissolving shavings of solid soap.

5 As a child, Gorbovsky lived, and had to fend for himself, for several years in the area occupied by Germany.

Gleb Gorbovsky

Роберт Рождественский

1932—1994

Ремонт часов

Сколько времени?
— Не знаю...
Что с часами?
— Непонятно...
То спешат они,
   показывая скорость не свою,
То, споткнувшись, останавливаются.
Только обоняньем
я примерно-приблизительное время узнаю...
Я сегодня подойду
   к одинокому еврею.
(Там на площади будочки выстроились в ряд.)
«Гражданин часовщик,
   почините мне время.
Что-то часики мои барахлят...»
Он, газету отложив,
на часы посмотрит внятно.
Покачает головою.
Снова глянет сверху вниз.
«Ай-яй-яй! —
   он мне скажет, —
Ай-яй-яй! Это ж надо!
До чего же вы, товарищ,
   довели механизм...
Может, это не нарочно.
Может, это вы нечаянно.
Для него — для механизма —
   абсолютно всё равно!
Вы совсем не бережете ваше время,
   ваши часики.
Сколько лет вы их не чистили?
То-то и оно!..»

Robert Rozhdestvensky

1932–1994

THE WATCHMAKER

What's the time?
– I've no idea.
Does this watch…
– I do not know:
It is fast sometimes,
      it clocks a speed above its proper pace.
And sometimes it stops completely;
that's when only by my nose
do I sense, though not too accurately, time in every case.
So today I will pop in
      to a lonely Jewish person.
(There are cabins in the square in the tradesmen's row.)
"Mr Watchmaker, please,
      fix my time, it is irksome
when one's watch is misbehaving quite so…"
He will put his book aside,
and will take my watch asunder,
shake his head and look it over,
up and down, then once again.
"Oy, oy-oy, –
      he will say then –
oy, oy-oy, it's no wonder:
for this timepiece, Mr Poet,
      you have been quite a bane.
Ah, so what – you didn't know?
Ah, so what – you are not like this?
It is all the same for clockworks
      once the maintenance has lapsed.
You've no care for your time,
        nor for this neglected timepiece.
Just how many years since you, Sir,
had it serviced last?"

Разберет часы потом он,
           причитая очень грозно.
И закончит, подышав на треугольную печать:
«Судя по часам „Москва",
вы уже довольно взрослый.
И пора уже
           за собственное время отвечать...»

Я скажу ему: «Спасибо!»
Выну пятьдесят копеек.
Тысяча семьсот шагов до знакомого двора.
И машины мне навстречу
           будут мчаться в брызгах пенных.
Будто это не машины.
Будто это глиссера́.[1]
Разлохмаченные листья прицепятся к ботинкам.
Станет улица качаться в неоновом огне...

А часы на руке будут тикать.
Тихо тикать.
И отсчитывать время,
предназначенное мне.

Robert Rozhdestvensky

He will clean and oil the clockwork,
        while continuing to growl,
and he'll stamp the log book, having signed it neatly on the line.
"Judging by the brand Moskvá,
you're already rather grown,
and it's time you felt
        responsible for your own time."

I will rise to say my thank-yous,
pay small change for all his toiling.
Seven hundred paces later, a familiar crossroads.
And there roaring cars will pass me
        splattering their foamy volleys.
As if they weren't really autos.
As if they were jet speedboats.
Wet and mangled matted leaves to my boot soles will be sticking,
and the pavement will be rocking to the neon symphony.

And the watch on my wrist will be ticking,
quietly ticking,
counting down the time beats
that have been assigned to me.

ПРОГНОЗ ПОГОДЫ

...В Нечерноземье, — согласно прогнозу, — [2]
резко уменьшится снежный покров...
Днем над столицей

                    местами — грозы.
А на асфальте
местами —
кровь.

1993(?)

WEATHER BULLETIN [3]

– Down in the west towards late-evening hours
rains are expected, there's risk of a flood...
By day in the capital
                            scattered showers,
and on the tarmac
some scattered
blood.

1993(?)

Notes

[1] The normative plural form of the word глиссер (speedboat, derived from the French glisseur) is глиссеры. The -á pattern occurs from time to time in masculine nouns as an alternative norm, professional usage or a colloquialism: for example, both трáкторы and тракторá are correct as the plural form of the word трактор (tractor).

[2] Нечерноземье is the north-western geographical region of Russia which includes both Moscow and St Petersburg. The literal meaning of its name is "non-black soil area".

[3] The poem starts in strict dactyl but deviates from it in lines 3–4. This is reflected in the translation.

Андрей Вознесенский

р. 1933

Ночной аэропорт в Нью-Йорке

Фасад

Автопортрет мой, реторта неона, апостол
$\qquad\qquad\qquad\qquad$ небесных ворот —
аэропорт!

Брезжат дюралевые витражи,
точно рентгентовский снимок души.
Как это страшно, когда в тебе небо стоит
в тлеющих трассах
необыкновенных столиц!

Каждые сутки
$\qquad\qquad\qquad$ тебя наполняют, как шлюз,
звездные судьбы
грузчиков, шлюх.

В баре, как ангелы, гаснут твои алкоголики.
Ты им глаголишь! [1]

Ты их, прибитых,
$\qquad\qquad\qquad$ возвышаешь.
Ты им «Прибытье»
$\qquad\qquad\qquad$ возвещаешь!

Летное поле

Ждут кавалеров, судеб, чемоданов, чудес…
Пять «Каравелл»
$\qquad\qquad\qquad$ ослепительно
$\qquad\qquad\qquad\qquad\qquad$ сядут с небес!
Пять полуночниц шасси выпускают устало.
Где же шестая?

Andrey Voznesensky

b.1933

A New York Airport at Night [2]

Façade [3]

You're my self-portrait, a neon retort, and a portal
                              that leads heavenward,
Airport!

In you, duralumin windows aglow
look like a giant X-ray of a soul.
It must be frightening holding inside you the sky's
smoldering trails
of extraordinary capital sites!

Flooded you are
                    like a lock, days and evenings, with scores
of the star-blessed:
baggage handlers and whores.

Down at the bar always hover your pale alcoholics
like angels fallen!

Them, humble, lowly,
                    you elevate.
To them the Arrival
                    you annunciate!

Airfield

Everyone's waiting for baggage, companions and fate...
Five Caravelles [4]
              so bedazzling
                        a landing will make!
Now each night-owl can let down all her tired undercarriage.
Five... one's not coming!

Видно, допрыгалась —
                    дрянь, аистенок, звезда!..
Электроплитками
                    пляшут под ней города.

Где она реет,
                    стонет, дурит?
И сигареткой
                    в тумане горит?..

Она прогноз не понимает.
Ее земля не принимает.

Интерьер

Худы прогнозы. И ты в ожидании бури,
как в партизаны, уходишь в свои вестибюли.
Мощное око взирает в иные мира́.[5]
Мойщики окон
                    слезят тебя, как мошкара,
звездный десантник, хрустальное чудище,
сладко, досадно быть сыном будущего,
где нет дураков
                    и вокзалов-тортов —
одни поэты и аэропорты!
Стонет в аквариумном стекле
небо,
          приваренное к земле.

Конструкции

Аэропорт — озона и солнца
аккредитованное посольство!

Сто поколений
                    не смели такого коснуться —
преодоленья
                    несущих конструкций.
Вместо каменных истуканов
стынет стакан синевы —
                    без стакана.

Serves you right, sixth one:

you storklet, you starlet, you oaf!

Cities beneath her are

rocking electrical stoves.[6]

Where is she frolicking,

soaring and fleeing?

Where is her roll-up

in fog smoldering?

She heard no forecast for the night.
Her landing clearance is denied.

Interior

Vile are the forecasts. And you – while expecting a tempest –
move, like guerrillas to strongholds, to your travel centers.
And, while your powerful eye seeks the worlds one can't reach,
each window cleaner

draws tears out of it like a midge.

You, paratrooper from space, crystal fixture,
it's bitter-sweet being a son of a Future
where there's no dumb-heads,

no stations-follies,

but only airports and poets!
Whimpers the windows' transparent girth:
heaven

arc-welded down to earth.

Structures

Airport: an Ozone-and-Sol state
fully accredited consulate!

Ten generations

weren't bold enough so as to trust this:

elimination

of load-bearing structures,

ditching a clutch of stone idols
for a glassful, sans the glass,

of cold sky-blue.

Рядом с кассами-теремами
он, точно газ,

                антиматериален!
Бруклин — дурак, твердокаменный черт.

Памятник эры —
аэропорт.

1961

Next to ticket parlors palatial,
it is, like gas,
                anti-experiential!
Brooklyn's contraption is hell's stony wart.

Our time's epitome
is an airport.[7]

1961

* * *

Мужчины с черными раскрытыми зонтами,
с сухими мыслями и мокрыми задами,
куда несетесь вы бессмысленною ночью
на черных парусах, пираты-одиночки?

Удача ваша, что вам молодость сулила,
прошла, горизонтальная, над вами —
как велосипед сюрреалиста —
вращаясь спицами под вашими зонтами.

* * *

Men rushing off, late, under flapping black umbrellas,
complete with sere thoughts and soggy underbellies,
where are you off to now amidst the weather's meanness,
under black sails at night, you solo buccaneers?

The lucky streak about which youth once made you pledges
has passed you overhead – a flatwise flying vélo,
a unicycle from surrealistic sketches –
its shiny spokes revolving under your umbrellas.

Notes

¹ See note 1 on p. 130. The normative spelling of the present-tense second-person singular form of this verb is глаголешь (first conjugation).

² The form of the original is simple yet unusual. The metre is dactyl with minor deviations (mainly in the final couplets of the first three parts), but the number of feet per line ranges from 2 to 7, with both extremes occurring in the first two lines of the poem. The rhyme scheme is straightforward couplets, but rhymes can be masculine, feminine, dactylic or even hybrid: алкоголики (which has a dactylic ending) is rhymed with глаголишь (feminine ending) and чудище (dactylic) with будущего (hyperdactylic ´ ⌣⌣⌣).

³ Voznesensky was trained as an architect, and it shows in many of his works.

⁴ The French SE 210 Caravelle was the first widely adopted jet airliner, whose introduction caused quite a stir.

⁵ Мирá is an irregular form which follows the colloquial -á pattern of plural forms. The correct plural accusative of мир (world) is миры́. However, the resulting rhyme is so convincing that this irregularity usually goes unnoticed by native speakers. See also note 1 on p. 184.

⁶ The image, easily lost on a contemporary reader, is that of an old-fashioned electrical stove. They had an exposed, hot-glowing heating element laid in a zigzag fashion into parallel grooves in a ceramic base.

⁷ Voznesensky is arguing with 'The Brooklyn Bridge' by Vladimir Mayakovsky (see pp. 55–63).

At the same time, 'A New York Airport at Night' pays a tongue-in-cheek tribute to Mayakovsky's stylistic legacy in its extensive – even by Voznesensky's standards – use of mosaic rhymes (some of which are internal or even initial here) and alliteration, to which the translation provides a few hints. The stepladder layout (seldom used by Voznesensky elsewhere) appears to be yet another nod to Mayakovsky. So may be the use of hybrid rhymes mentioned in note 2 above: there are as many as five instances of them in 'The Brooklyn Bridge' where the rhyme scheme is αβαβ. However, such rhymes occasionally occur in other works by Voznesensky and do not necessarily constitute a deliberate stylisation here.

'A New York Airport at Night' and 'The Brooklyn Bridge' are also obviously linked by the shared theme of a visitor marvelling at a technological wonder of the world.

Евгений Евтушенко

р. 1933

* * *

Л. Мартынову

Окно выходит в белые деревья.
Профессор долго смотрит на деревья.
Он очень долго смотрит на деревья
и очень долго мел крошит в руке.
Ведь это просто — правила деленья!
А он забыл их —

правила деленья!
Забыл —

подумать —

правила деленья!
Ошибка! Да! Ошибка на доске!

Мы все сидим сегодня по-другому,
и слушаем и смотрим по-другому,
да и нельзя сейчас не по-другому,
и нам подсказка в этом не нужна.
Ушла жена профессора из дому.
Не знаем мы,

куда ушла из дому,
не знаем,

отчего ушла из дому,
а знаем только, что ушла она.

В костюме и немодном и неновом, —
как и всегда, немодном и неновом, —
да, как всегда, немодном и неновом, —
спускается профессор в гардероб.
Он долго по карманам ищет номер:
«Ну что такое?

Где же этот номер?

Yevgeny Yevtushenko

b.1933

* * *

To L. Martynov[1]

All windows here command a view of white trees.
The Latin teacher looking at the white trees,
his gaze is long and steady on the white trees,
his hand takes just as long to crush the chalk.
What plural ending should he use with *fratris*?[2]
He's always known
               that plural form of *fratris*...
Imagine,
      to forget
             what goes with *fratris*!
An error! On the blackboard! In that block!

After the bell we stay without a moan,
we watch and listen, all without a moan,
we have to be this way, we must not moan,
we need no prompting to perceive the heft.
We know the teacher's wife has left their home
but not who for
             she left their married home,
but not the reason why
               she left their home –
indeed, all that we know is that she's left.

His suit is old; it is so not in fashion,
perennially old and not in fashion,
it is indeed completely out of fashion;
and at the checkroom on his way he calls.
He's searching in his pocket for the hat check
"Oh what is it,
           where is this goddamn hat check?

А может быть,

                  не брал у вас я номер?

Куда он делся? —

              Трет рукою лоб. —

Ах, вот он!..

        Что ж,

             как видно, я старею,

Не спорьте, тетя Маша,

           я старею.

И что уж тут поделаешь —

           старею...»

Мы слышим — дверь внизу скрипит за ним.

Окно выходит в белые деревья,

в большие и красивые деревья,

но мы сейчас глядим не на деревья,

мы молча на профессора глядим.

Уходит он,

       сутулый,

              неумелый,

какой-то

        беззащитно-неумелый,

я бы сказал —

           устало-неумелый,

под снегом,

         мягко падающим в тишь.

Уже и сам он,

        как деревья,

              белый,

да,

   как деревья,

          совершенно белый,

еще немного —

         и настолько белый,

что среди них

       его не разглядишь.

1955

Perhaps I left my hat
                    and took no hat check?"
He rubs his forehead
                    trying to recall.

"Ah here it is!..
                    I'm getting absent-minded.
I'm getting older, Jane,
                    and absent-minded.
Don't argue,
          I am old
                    and absent-minded..."
He steps outside into the winter cold.
All windows here command a view of white trees;
they're large and beautiful, those stately white trees,
but we, we are not looking at the white trees
since it's our teacher that we all behold.

He walks away;
               he's stooped
                    but also knightly.
He looks defenseless,
                    but still also knightly.
Or I would say,
               fatigued but also knightly
under the snowflakes'
                    silent twirl and twist.
He's
     like the trees,
                    already full of whiteness,
like all those trees
               he's full
                    of quiet whiteness,
another moment –
               full of so much whiteness
that one could not descry him
                    in their midst.

1955

* * *

К. Шульженко

А снег повалится, повалится,
и я прочту в его канве,
что моя молодость повадится
опять заглядывать ко мне.

И поведет куда-то за руку,
на чьи-то тени и шаги,
и вовлечет в старинный заговор
огней, деревьев и пурги.

И мне покажется, покажется
по Сре́тенкам и Мохо́вым,[3]
что молод не был я пока еще,
а только буду молодым.

И ночь завертится, завертится
и, как в воронку, втянет в грех,
и моя молодость завесится
со мною снегом ото всех.

Но, сразу ставшая накрашенной
при беспристрастном свете дня,
цыганкой, мною наигравшейся,
оставит молодость меня.

Начну я жизнь переиначивать,
свою наивность застыжу
и сам себя, как пса бродячего,
на цепь угрюмо посажу.

Но снег повалится, повалится,
закружит всё веретеном,
и моя молодость появится
опять цыганкой под окном.

А снег повалится, повалится,
и цепи я перегрызу,
и жизнь, как снежный ком, покатится
к сапожкам чьим-то там, внизу.

* * *

to K. Shulzhenko [4]

Then snow will fall, and it will powder,
and I'll divine from its long twines
that soon my youth will come around and
will keep returning for a while.

She'll come and lead me by the hand towards
somebody's shadows and footsteps.
And she will leave me in the Camelots
of lights and trees and blizzard nets.

I'll have the feeling, when I follow
from street to street her paces sprung,
that I've not yet been a young fellow,
that I am only to be young.

The night will play along with wanderlust
as angst my reason circumscribes.
My youth and I will screen the two of us
with thick snow drapes from prying eyes.

But when the ruthless day illuminates
my youth's cosmetic overlay,
I, like a gypsy woman's clueless mate,
will be abandoned after play.

I'll try to change my life all o'er again
ashamed of being so naive.
I'll chain myself down to a lonely den,
a treatment headstrong dogs receive.

But snow will fall, and it will powder,
a blizzard spinning on its core.
My youth once more will come around then,
a gypsy woman by the door.

And snow will fall and it will powder,
and I shall gnaw off all the chains,
and growing, like a snowball, rounder
my life will roll down snow-swept lanes.

Notes

[1] Leonid Martynov, a poet included in this anthology.

[2] In the original he is a professor and has forgotten "the rules of division". This substitution is discussed on p. xliv.

[3] Сретенка and Моховая are streets in the historic centre of Moscow.

[4] Klavdiya Shulzhenko (1906–1984), a famous singer and actress. Her repertoire in the 1970s included a song with lyrics by Yevtushenko.

Всеволод Некрасов

1934—2009

И Я ПРО КОСМИЧЕСКОЕ

Полечу или нет — не знаю
До луны или до звезды
Но луну я пробовал на язык
В сорок первом году в Казани

Затемнение
война
тем не менее
луна

Белый
свет

Белый
снег

Белый
хлеб
которого нет

никакого нет

Я давным-давно вернулся в Москву
Я почти каждый день обедаю

А на вид луна была вкусная
А на вкус луна была белая

1959

Vsevolod Nekrasov

1934–2009

On Cosmos, from Me, Too

Will I fly, will I not? – can't fathom
Will I fly to the Moon, to stars?
But I tasted the Moon on my tongue
In 1941, in Kazan [1]

Full blackouts
war goons
it them flouts
the moon

White
glow

White
snow

White
bread
last seen long ago

very long ago

Years have passed since I returned to Moscow
Now I eat dinner almost every night [2]

Yet the Moon to me looked ambrosial
Yet the Moon to me tasted brilliant white [3]

1959

* * *

Сотри случайные черты

Три четыре

Сотри случайные черты

Смотри случайно
не протри только
дырочки

* * *

Erase the features Chance installed [4]

Raise let fall

Erase the features Chance installed

Watch by chance
do not rub
a hole

Notes

[1] Kazan (Казань) is a city in the east of European Russia which served as a major safe haven for evacuees during World War II.

[2] These two lines are a rare example of syllabic verse in Russian poetry. The translation reproduces their 10-syllable shape.

[3] The corresponding two lines of the original are written in the 5+5 folk-verse metre ∪∪–∪∪ ∪∪–∪∪ (see also note 4 on p. 262) which has a characteristic intonation, emphasised here by the anaphora and grammatical parallelism. At the same time, they keep the syllable count of the previous two (syllabic) lines with which they rhyme.

[4] Nekrasov is arguing with famous verses by Alexander Blok from which this whole line is quoted:

> Жизнь — без начала и конца.
> Нас всех подстерегает случай.
> Над нами — сумрак неминучий
> Иль ясность божьего лица.
> Но ты, художник, твердо веруй
> В начала и концы. Ты знай,
> Где стерегут нас ад и рай.
> Тебе дано бесстрастной мерой
> Измерить всё, что видишь ты.
> Твой взгляд — да будет твёрд и ясен,
> Сотри случайные черты —
> И ты увидишь: мир прекрасен.

> •

> Life seeks a multitude of ends,
> With everyone Chance seeks a meeting,
> Above us darkness unremitting
> Beside God's lucid countenance.
> Despite this, keep your faith, oh artist,
> In structure. Let your gift innate,
> Where hell and heaven lie in wait,
> Apply dispassionately yardsticks
> To everything that you behold.
> Your sight be lucid, steeped in duty,
> Erase the features Chance installed,
> And you will see the world's great beauty.

The original has end rhymes (черты-четыре), initial rhymes (сотри-три-смотри), a rhyming word in the middle of a line (протри), a sonority between дырочки and "сотри черты"-"три четыре" and a deliberate repetition случайные-случайно. The translation attempts to do justice to these features.

In the ultimate blackness

в последнюю темень

Евгений Рейн

р. 1935

Подпись к разорванному портрету

Глядя на краны, речные трамваи,
Парусники, сухогрузы, моторки,
Я и тебя, и тебя вспоминаю,
Помню, как стало легко без мотовки,
Лгуньи, притворщицы, неженки, злюки,
Преобразившей Васильевский остров
В землю свиданья и гавань разлуки.
Вздох облегченья и бешенства воздух…
Годы тебя не украсили тенью,
Алой помадой по розовой коже.
Я тебя помню в слезах нетерпенья.
О, не меняйся! И сам я такой же!
Я с высоты этой многоэтажной
Вижу не только залив и заводы,
Мне открывается хронос протяжный
И выставляет ушедшие годы.
Вижу я комнат чудно́е убранство:
Фотопортреты, букеты, флаконы.
Всё, что мы делали, было напрасно —
Нам не оплатят ни дни, ни прогоны.[1]
Глядя отсюда, не жаль позолоты
Зимнему дню, что смеркается рано.
Выжили только одни разговоры,
Словно за пазухой у Эккермана.[2]
Как ты похожа лицом-циферблатом,
Прыткая муза истории Клио,
На эту девочку с вычурным бантом,
Жившую столь исступленно и криво
В скомканном времени, в доме нечистом,
В неразберихе надсады и дрожи.
Ключик полночный, кольцо с аметистом,
Туфли единственные, и всё же

Evgeny Rein

b.1935

The Caption to a Rent Portrait

Seeing the cranes and the trams-of-the-river,
Sailing yachts, tugs and self-rigged outboard motors,
I keep recalling you, over and over,
And the respite from a cheat and a rotten
Shrew, whose pretence was a match for her malice,
But who transformed the Vasílyevsky island [3]
Into a harbor of meeting and heartbreak.
Sighs of relief and the air full of ire...
Years that have passed left no shade on your face and
No scarlet lipstick, the skin fresh and rosy.
I can remember your tears of impatience.
Please, do not change! I am still who I was then!
From the apartment-block high-level vantage
I watch the Gulf and the works, but not only: [4]
There's also Cronos's own stretched-out vastness
Making display of the years that have gone by.
There I behold rooms with quaint decorations:
Photographed portraits, bouquets, perfume phials.
All that we did was so totally wasteful:
No-one will pay our per diem and mileage.
Looking from here, who'd begrudge golden casting
To a short day in a long winter season?
Nothing survived but our lengthy discussions,
As if recorded by Goethe's assistant.
Clio, the History Muse with her slow
Face-dial, quick beyond all expectations,
Looks like this girl with a fanciful bow,
Who used to live in some warped exaltation,
In crumpled time and a home less than cleanly,
The trembling of self-induced overstretching.
Keys to a night door, an amethyst pendant,
Shoes, the one pair that she had then, and yet she

Даже вино, что всегда наготове,
Даже с гусиною кожицей эрос
Предпочитала законной любови,[5]
Вечно впадая то в ярость, то в ересь.
Если вглядеться в последнюю темень,
Свет ночника вырывает из мрака
Бешеной нежности высшую степень —
В жизни, как в письмах, помарки с размаха.

Rather preferred to a love good and proper
Even the wine, always kept at the ready,
Even the eros – goosebumpy, not raucous, –
Getting alternately mad and heretic.
Peering at length in the ultimate blackness,
One can discern in the murk, night-lamp spotlit,
Furious tenderness topping all rankings.
Life's like a letter: a sweeping hand blots it.

В ТЕМНОМ БЛЕСКЕ

Н.

По железу ранним утром в темном блеске
чешет дождь, я поднимаю занавески.[6]
Вот он, мой неотвратимый серый город,
дождь идет, как заводной и верный робот.
Ну, чего тебе в такое утро надо,
ранней осени бессмертная прохлада,
поздней жизни перекопанная нива,
линза света — переменчивое диво?
Здесь и зелень, и багряно-золотое,
мел и темень, да и прочее любое.
Всё, что было, всё, что стало и пропало:
думал — хватит, а выходит — мало, мало!
Пусть идет он, этот дождик, до полудня,
да и вечером, и ночью — вот и чу́дно!
Пусть размочит, размягчит сухую корку,
пусть войдет до самой смерти в поговорку.[7]
И пока он льет, не зная перерыва,
всё, что было, поправимо, нежно, живо.

Evgeny Rein

DARKLING GLITTER

To N. [8]

Rain is falling – early morning, darkling glitter –
rapping on the corrugated roof and gutter.
In the window frame my city's grey and stolid,
rain drops working as a faultless wind-up robot.
What on earth do you expect of such a morning,
early autumn with your deathless, cooling fore wind;
later life with your recultivated garden;
lens of sunlight – a capricious willful wonder?
Here are colors: green and gold with ancient purple,[9]
soot with chalk and all you need for any purpose.
All that was, and all that is, and all that's vanished –
I thought: that's enough, but now I'm famished, famished!
May this rain go on and on throughout the morning,
then the afternoon, the evening, I'm not groaning!
May it melt the hardened crust, dried-up and dour,
may eternity elapse over its hour.
And as long as it pours on and knows no resting
all that was is live, redeemable, caressing.

Notes

[1] Here, прогоны means travel expenses.

[2] Johann Peter Eckermann (1792–1854), German writer known mainly as the assistant of the ageing Goethe and the author of the memoir *Gespräche mit Goethe in den letzten Jahren seines Lebens,* 1823–32.

[3] Vasilyevsky (Васильевский) island forms part of the historic centre of St Petersburg.

[4] Much of St Petersburg's heavy industry is located on, or near, the shore of the Gulf of Finland.

[5] Любови is a poetic variant of the genitive, dative and prepositional cases of the word любовь (love). It is unusual for Rein to use this form, although some poets, notably Bulat Okudzhava (who is included in this anthology) seem to prefer it to the normative form: любви.

[6] The verb чесать is used here in its figurative meaning. When used this way, it designates an implied action performed with a particular vigour.

[7] This line combines two idioms: "войти в поговорку" (to become famous or infamous; literally, "to enter a proverb") and "до самой смерти" (forever; literally, "until the very death").

[8] Apparently Nadezhda Rein, the poet's wife.

[9] The colour of turning leaves (багряный, багрец – not to be confused with багровый which is darker and has a bluish hue) has been mentioned by Pushkin in his celebrated poems describing autumn. On at least one occasion it occurs in combination with the golden colour: "в багрец и золото одетые леса" (woods dressed in ancient purple and gold). This precise combination "багряно-золотое" (ancient purple with gold) in the original of 'Darkling Glitter' is likely to be a deliberate reference to Pushkin's vision of autumn.

"Ancient purple" is an approximation of the colour described by багряный/багрец, the latter being redder and brighter. English translations from Pushkin variously render it as "purple", "crimson" or "scarlet", none of which does full justice to the colour either. The word багряный is based on an ancient Slavic root, which gives it an old-fashioned and noble character in modern Russian. "Ancient purple" captures this aspect better than the alternative descriptions.

Олжас Сулейменов

р. 1936

ОКРАИНА

Когда жара сойдет
                    до теплоты,
фонарь согнется под вечерней ношей
и слабым отрицаньем темноты
свет верно служит азиатской ночи,
иду туда, где точки папирос
со всех сторон кошачьими зрачками,
где в мае по спине моей — мороз,
где жизнь — копейка, если не нахален.
Здесь сладко пахнет старым воровством,
на седла брошенным девичьим вскриком.
Окраиной души горжусь родством
с негромкой, дикой слободскою кликой.

Темно, движенья белые видны,
скамейка занята, на ней колдуют —
ух, женщина ему за ворот дует,
сорочку отдирая от спины.

Взошла луна.
В тиши журчит вода.
Собака спит. Спит сторож с алебардой.
Под яблоней — забытая лопата.
И овощной ларек,
                    закрытый навсегда.

Olzhas Suleimenov

b.1936

OUTER LIMITS

The midday heat will turn
                 into mere warmth.[1]
The evening load will bend the lampposts forward.
A weak denial of the dark on earth,
street light is Asian night's obedient servant.
I'm in a place where *papirósa* points [2]
are dotted everywhere – a cat's eye glare, –
where though it's May I shiver in my bones,
where life is cheap, unless you push and dare.
This old place has a sweet abduction smell,
an echo of a girl's scream over saddles.
The outer limits of my soul still swell
with kinship to this wild, free-settler rabble.

It's dark; still one can see a moving shape,
that of a couple on a park bench fooling:
hey-ho, she blows upon his neck to cool it
while peeling off his collar from the nape.

The moon is up.
The warbling waters pour.
A dog's curled up. A guard naps with his halberd.
Under an apple tree a laid-down shovel.[3]
A veggie stall
               that's closed forevermore.

* * *

Кто-то медленно скачет и скачет во сне,
издалёка, на светлом усталом коне.
Всё молчит. Осторожно копыта стучат.
Скачешь ты
или тихо крадешься ко мне?
Почему не взлетает над крупом камча́? [4]
Почему ты являешься мне по ночам?
Я поверю,
я знаю — ты добрый гонец!
Почему же так тихо копыта стучат?

Olzhas Suleimenov

* * *

Every night someone steadily rides through my dream [5]
from afar, on the back of a stallion-gleam.
All is silence, the slow-moving hooves barely thump.
Are you riding to me,
or perhaps sneaking in?
Why does not your whip cord rise and fall on the rump?
Why do you come at night when I turn off the lamp?
I'll believe you,
good messenger, you're not a fiend!
So why then should the hooves almost noiselessly thump?

Notes

[1] This is intended as a joke, similar to "ordered to wait till what was officially called the cool of the evening…" in Rudyard Kipling's 'Love-o'-Women'.

[2] *Papirosas* are a kind of cigarettes: see note 5 on p. 150.

[3] The setting of this poem is the suburbs of Alma-Ata (now spelled Almaty) which is situated in an oasis-like area famous for its apples. There are many orchards on the outskirts of the city.

[4] Камча is an Asian-style riding whip.

[5] The form of this poem is discussed on p. xx.

Александр Кушнер

р. 1936

* * *

Четко вижу двенадцатый век.
Два-три моря да несколько рек.
Крикнешь здесь — там услышат твой голос.

Так что ласточки в клюве могли
Занести, обогнав корабли,
В Корнуэльс из Ирландии волос.

А сейчас что за век, что за тьма!
Где письмо? Не дождаться письма.
Даром волны шумят, набегая.

Иль и впрямь европейский роман
Отменен, похоронен Тристан?
Или ласточек нет, дорогая?

Alexander Kushner

b.1936

* * *

I can see the twelfth century well:
A few seas surge, a few rivers swell.
Cry out here, they will hear over there.

So that swallows could carry with ease –
Overtaking all boats on the seas –
A long hair to west Cornwall from Eire.

And how now, when the age is so dark?
Hopes for post... Their forlornness is marked,
And in vain sways the swell by the pier.

Is it true that in Europe romance
Is *passé*, Tristan looked at askance?
Or have swallows now vanished, my dear?

* * *

Этот мальчик в коротких штанишках,
С общепринятым плюшевым мишкой,
Толстобрюхого друга ему,
Сразу видно, всучили, — формально
Держит зверя за лапу, печально
Смотрит в непроходимую тьму.

Стыдно мне его умного взгляда.
Он снимается: надо — так надо.
Из далекого, детского дня
Подневольного, — если бы рая! —
Деликатный, с трудом узнавая,
С жалостью он глядит на меня.

Alexander Kushner

* * *

This young boy with a sad broody stare
Facing darkness, and that teddy bear –
Not a toy, but a studio prop...
A traditional set for a photo:
He is dutiful, pinching a paw toe
As he waits for the birdie to pop.

I'm ashamed at his eyes' inner glow.
He is posing – as ordered, I know.
From a life, which back then had to be
A dependent one – hardly a nice thing! –
He is looking, not quite recognising,
With a delicate pity – at me.

Юнна Мориц

р. 1937

* * *

Страна вагонная, вагонное терпенье,
вагонная поэзия и пенье,
вагонное родство и воровство,
ходьба враскачку, сплетни, анекдоты,
впадая в спячку, забываешь — кто ты,
вагонный груз, людское вещество,
тебя везут, жара, обходчик в майке
гремит ключом, завинчивая гайки,
тебя везут, мороз, окно во льду,
и непроглядно — кто там в белой стуже
гремит ключом, затягивая туже
всё те же гайки... Втянутый в езду,
в ее крутые яйца и галеты,
в ее пейзажи — забываешь, где ты,
и вдруг осатанелый проводник
кулачным стуком, окриком за дверью,
тоску и радость выдыхая зверью,
велит содрать постель!.. И в тот же миг,
о верхнюю башкой ударясь полку,
себя находишь — как в стогу иголку,
и молишься, о Боже, помоги
переступить зиянье в две ладони,
когда застынет поезд на перроне
и страшные в глазах пойдут круги.

Yunna Morits

b.1937

* * *

The land of wagons-lits, with wagon-patience,
with wagon-verse and singing on occasions,
with wagon-kinship and with petty theft;
there's waddle, gossip, funny stories, humdrum
(you hibernate, forgetting where you come from) –
a wagon-cargo of some human weft.
A siding, swelter; one bare-chested trackman
is tightening rail nuts, his spanner rattling;
a siding, winter cold, thick window frost –
it's hard to see: who *is* this snowy blighter,
whose spanner rattles screwing down yet tighter
the same old nuts... You're very much engrossed
in journeying: its hardboiled eggs and canned food
(its vistas, too), forgetting where you've come to;
then the conductor as if straight from hell
barks in the corridor while banging fiercely,
exhaling torment, jubilation beastly:
"All strip your bedding!"... You at once, as well,
administer the upper berth a head whack,
locate yourself – a needle in a haystack,
and there you are: in need of heaven's grace
to straddle the glaring gap of seven inches
when finally the brakes complete their screeches
and stars across your vision start to race.

Yunna Morits writes both for adults and for children and, accordingly,
possesses two completely different poetic personalities. The format of
the anthology compelled us to select one poem from each category
even though they would not normally be mixed under the same cover.
These two works should be considered in isolation from each other, as
if written by different authors.

КОТ-МОРЕХОД

Жил в Одессе черный кот,
Он залез на пароход,
С удовольствием в буфете
Съел с колбаской бутерброд,
Лапой дверь открыл в каюту
И улегся на минуту.

В это время кочегар
Сделал в топке сильный жар,
Боцман свистнул —
И матросы
Отвязали быстро тросы
И отплыли из Одессы
Прямо на Мадагаскар!

Пароход качался плавно,
Черный кот проспался славно
И, очнувшись через сутки,
Он мяукнул:
— Что за шутки?!
Обожают плавать утки,
Сельди, лебеди и гуси,
Но в моем ли это вкусе?
Сухопутному коту
Хорошо гулять в порту,
Но гулять по океану,
Извините, я не стану!

Всем известно, что коты
Могут прыгать с высоты,
Но не могут прыгать в воду
Сухопутные коты!
Пусть немедленно матрос
Размотает крепкий трос
И привяжет пароход,
Чтоб сошел на землю кот!

Но сказал матрос коту:
— Ты остался на борту!

Seafaring Tom

In Odessa a black cat[1]
Crept aboard a steamer yacht.
He regaled himself with sausage
Deep within the galley's glut,
To a cabin sneaked and in it
He lay down for just a minute.

That's when by the engine beam
Mr Stoker raised the steam,
Mr Boatswain blew his whistle,
In
    the mooring lines went swiftly,
And the yacht sailed from Odessa
For the West Pacific Rim![2]

Gently was the steam yacht swaying,
And the cat enjoyed a lay in.
After twenty-four hours' lying
He awoke and bellowed:
"Blimey!
Ducks like travelling in water,
Swans and geese, a river otter;
That's the thing I am *not* hot for!
Surely a landfaring cat
By the quayside should be sat.
Placing me amidst an ocean
Is a scandalous demotion!

Cats can jump, and be alright,
From a rather daunting height
Onto anything but water:
They are the landfaring kind!
Mr Seaman, would you like
To unwind the mooring line,
Tether up the steamer yacht,
So that he may land, the cat."

Mr Seaman in retort:
"Why, you chose to stay on board!

Погляди по сторонам!
Мы несемся по волнам,
А к волнам, любезный кот,
Не привяжешь пароход!
Ты теперь — не пешеход,
А отважный мореход!

Вот привязана корзинка
К белой мачте корабля,
А в корзинке —
Черный-черный
Кот сидит с трубой подзорной:
Смотрит — скоро ли земля?

Look around you, cast your gaze:
We are gliding on the waves,
And one couldn't, my dear cat
Tether to the waves the yacht.
You no longer walk the land;
Seas you voyage and command!"

There's a wicker basket fastened
To the white mast with a band.
In the basket –
Black and sooty –
The seafaring cat is sitting,
With a spyglass: seeking land.

Notes

[1] Odessa is a city and a major port on the Black Sea.

[2] In the original the destination is Madagascar.

As if forever

думалось — навеки

Лев Лосев

1937—2009

Местоимения

Предательство, которое в крови.
Предать себя, предать свой глаз и палец,
предательство распутников и пьяниц,
но от иного, Боже, сохрани.

Вот мы лежим. Нам плохо. Мы больной.
Душа живет под форточкой отдельно.
Под нами не обычная постель, но
тюфяк-тухляк, больничный перегной.

Чем я, больной, так неприятен мне,
так это тем, что он такой неряха:
на морде пятна супа, пятна страха
и пятна чёрт чего на простыне.[1]

Еще толчками что-то в нас течет,
когда лежим с озябшими ногами,
и всё, что мы за жизнь свою налгали,
теперь нам предъявляет длинный счет.

Но странно и свободно ты живешь
под форточкой, где ветка, снег и птица,
следя, как умирает эта ложь,
как больно ей и как она боится.

Lev Loseff

1937–2009

PRONOUNS

The treachery that runs through one's own blood.
To self-betray, betray one's eye, one's finger...
Betrayals of a lech, a heavy drinker –
and if another kind, have mercy, God.

There. We're bedridden. We is quite so ill.[2]
Soul lives apart beneath the window's vent-flap.
Under our body isn't just a bed wrap:
a rotted mattress, hospital topsoil.

What I, a patient, so disgust me with
is the display of his being so untidy:
his snout in spots – of soup, and from anxiety;
his sheets in spots as well – of something worse.

Some fluid pulsates inside our vessels still,
when our wrapped feet feel so distinctly icy,
and all our lies, accrued since birth, are racing
to whack us with a rather hefty bill.

And yet how strangely, freely you abide
under the vent-flap, near birds, snow and air,
observing how this lie's about to die,
how it's in pain and filling up with fear.

* * *

Тяжко Сизифу катить камень на гору крутую.
То-то веселье зато с горки за камнем бежать!

* * *

Sisyphus labors so hard rolling his stone up the mountain...[3]
Yes, but it is such a joy running behind it downhill![4]

Notes

[1] "Черт чего" is a reduced form of the idiomatic "черт знает чего" (of the devil knows what).

[2] The use of pronouns in the original is intentionally ungrammatical.

[3] The form of the original is elegiac distich, unrhymed as it is supposed to be. The system of imitating duration-based classical metres in Russian syllabic-accentual verse was developed by Vasily Trediakovsky (1703–1768) and is similar to the approach adopted in English and German prosodies. The metrical scheme in this case is

$$-\cup\cup \ -\cup\cup \ - \ \| \ -\cup\cup \ -\cup\cup \ -\cup$$
$$-\cup\cup \ -\cup\cup \ - \ \| \ -\cup\cup \ -\cup\cup \ -$$

To answer a frequently asked question: the first line utilises the freedom which is allowed in Russian hexameter and reflects the dactyl/spondee flexibility in certain feet of its classical prototype. In this case a pause is substituted for two unstressed syllables at the caesura:

$$-\cup\cup \ -\cup\cup \ -\wedge\wedge \ \| \ -\cup\cup \ -\cup\cup \ -\cup$$

So although the two lines of this poem are nearly identical metrically, the first qualifies as hexameter and the second as pentameter (following the traditional 2½+2½=5 logic of classical prosody where a long syllable is ascribed the same duration as two short syllables).

[4] The "up and down" theme, playing on the rising quality of the first line of an elegiac distich and the falling quality of the second, can be traced back to the poem by Friedrich Schiller which follows below, with its translation by Samuel Taylor Coleridge:

> Im Hexameter steigt des Springquells flüssige Säule,
> Im Pentameter drauf fällt sie melodisch herab.

> •

> In the hexameter rises the fountain's silvery column;
> In the pentameter, aye, falling in melody back.

Several Russian translations of this distich are available; the one by Efim Etkind (1918–1999) is particularly close to Loseff's poem in its metrical structure:

> Гордо в гекзаметре вверх взмывает колонна фонтана,
> Чтобы в пентаметре вновь звучно на землю упасть.

In 20th-century Russian poetry classical stylisations were more often than not used for ironic effect when dealing with distinctly non-classical matters. Here Loseff goes even further, mocking a classical subject and, to an extent, Schiller's poem which describes its own imitative classical form.

There is at least one more layer of meaning here: the poem appears as an epigraph to Loseff's book *Sisyphus Redux*, so it also reflects on his own writing in the same ironic key.

Владимир Высоцкий

1938—1980

Про дикого вепря

В королевстве, где всё тихо и складно,
Где ни войн, ни катаклизмов, ни бурь,
Появился дикий вепрь огромадный — [1]
То ли буйвол, то ли бык, то ли тур.

Сам король страдал желудком и астмой,
Только кашлем сильный страх наводил, —
А тем временем зверюга ужасный
Коих ел, а коих в лес волочил.[2]

И король тотчас издал три декрета:
«Зверя надо одолеть наконец!
Вот кто отчается на это, на это,[3]
Тот принцессу поведет под венец.»

А в отчаявшемся том государстве —
Как войдешь, так сразу наискосок —
В бесшабашной жил тоске и гусарстве
Бывший лучший, но опальный стрелок.

На полу лежали люди и шкуры,
Пели песни, пили меды — и тут
Протрубили во дворе трубадуры,
Хвать стрелка — и во дворец волокут.

И король ему прокашлял: «Не буду
Я читать тебе морали, юнец, —
Но если завтра победишь чуду-юду,[4]
То принцессу поведешь под венец.»

А стрелок: «Да это что за награда?!
Мне бы — выкатить портвейна бадью!»
Мол, принцессу мне и даром не надо, —
Чуду-юду я и так победю! [5]

Vladimir Vysotsky

1938–1980

THE BALLAD OF A VERY WILD BEAST [6]

To a kingdom, always happy and quiet,
unafflicted by storms, famines or war,
Came a beast that was as wild as a riot:
One half-human, half-bovine Minotaur.

There the King was but an old chronic patient,
Though his cough was known to make courtiers fall,
And the beast was of carnivorous persuasion
And exacted an immense human toll.

So the King at once dictated three orders:
"Beast be found and slain, that is my behest!
And he who's brave enough for this parlous slaughter
Shall be wed to no-one else but Princess."

As our King grew more depressed and changed colour,
Courtiers with some trepidation recalled
An irreverent hidalgo of valour,
Expert swordsman – who'd been banished from court.

Promptly heralds were dispatched to the forest,
And they dragged out of a humble abode
The King's warrior, though neglectful of mores,
Still unvanquished and quite lethal with sword.

And the King coughed with a great air of sorrow:
"Son, forget what may have happened before.
Thou shalt be wed to my sweet daughter tomorrow,
If by morn thou findst and slayst Minotaur!"

– "Let thy daughter go on being Royal Virgin.
This is surely not a decent reward!
From the kingdom's most expensive wine merchants
Thou shalt buy me one full barrel of Port."

А король: «Возьмешь принцессу — и точка!
А не то тебя раз-два — и в тюрьму!
Ведь это всё же королевская дочка!..»
А стрелок: «Ну хоть убей — не возьму!»

И пока король с ним так препирался,
Съел уже почти всех женщин и кур
И возле самого дворца ошивался
Этот самый то ли бык, то ли тур.

Делать нечего — портвейн он отспорил,
Чуду-юду уложил — и убёг...[7]
Вот так принцессу с королем опозорил
Бывший лучший, но опальный стрелок.

1966

And the King: "Still thou shalt marry the lady!
Lest I order thy dumb head on a plate.
Look, she hath been so very hopeful and ready…"
And the knight: "Then do behead me: 'tis fate."

While the two of them were raving and ranting,
Still at large our disagreeable beast
Was by the very castle keep gallivanting,
Having eaten near all women and geese.

No escape in sight. The barrel rolled out,
Minotaur was promptly put to the sword…
And thus dishonoured king and country our proud
Expert swordsman, who'd been banished from court.

1966

ПАДЕНИЕ АЛИСЫ

Догонит ли в воздухе — или шалишь — [8]
Летучая кошка летучую мышь?
Собака летучая — кошку летучую? [9]
Зачем я себя этой глупостью мучаю!

А раньше я думала, стоя над кручею:
Ах, как бы мне сделаться тучей летучею!
Ну вот я и стала летучею тучею,
Ну вот и решаю по этому случаю:

Догонит ли в воздухе — или шалишь —
Летучая кошка летучую мышь?

Vladimir Vysotsky

Down the Rabbit-Hole [10]

If bats were to flee from a feline that flies,
Would some end up caught, same as cats catching mice?
Could a... flying dog catch a cat, also flying?
Why ask myself silly things fit for a clown!

Once, stood at a brink and a wish being allowed,
I wished to be turned into a... flying cloud.
And now that I finally fly as a cloud
The question is constantly coming around:

If bats were to flee from a feline that flies,
Would some end up caught, same as cats catching mice?

Notes

1 Огромадный is a colloquial variant of громадный (huge).

2 Коих is the plural accusative form of кой, an archaic and literary relative conjunctive. The modern equivalent is который (masculine singular nominative), которых (plural accusative). The word is used here as part of the expression "коих ..., а коих ..." (here, "ate some and dragged the others to the forest") the modern form of which would be "одних ..., а других ...".

3 "Отчаяться на ..." means "to resort to the desperate act of ...", but it also has an archaic meaning "to muster courage for ...", which is what the king is saying here. This comical ambiguity is accentuated by the re-occurrence of the participle отчаявшийся in the first line of the next stanza, this time to describe the whole country.

4 The ailing King makes a mistake when inflecting a rare word. He treats the noun чудо-юдо (wonder beast) as if it were of the feminine gender, while it is actually neuter as evidenced by its -o ending, so its accusative case coincides with the nominative.

5 Further linguistic exuberance: a repetition of the King's mistake is followed by a humorous attempt to form the first-person singular future perfective form of the verb победить (meaning "to defeat" in this context: "I will defeat"/"I will have defeated"), which does not exist in Russian.

6 This is an adaptation of Vysotsky's lyrics. In order to capture the playful stylistics of the original, its meaning had to be modified more than would be appropriate in a conventional translation. The flavour of the original story is mock-medieval European, with details such as troubadours providing a hilarious counterpoint to the very Russian colloquial expressions, idioms and word play systematically used in the text. Burlesque Ancient Greek references were chosen to provide a similar counterpoint in the English version. The Minotaur story has all the essential characters: a vicious beast, a king, a hero, and a princess who eventually gets rejected. It is quite possible that Vysotsky used this story as a starting point, especially bearing in mind the bovine references in his description of the beast.

The general metre of the original is essentially the same logaoedic as in 'The Ballad of the Elderly People' by Alexander Galich (pp. 114–116): $-\cup\ -\cup\ \cup\cup-\ -\cup\ -(\cup)$, with the dominating rhythmic pattern ∪∪´∪ ∪∪´ ∪∪´(∪), except that here the even lines are truncated to masculine endings. The first foot occasionally starts with an additional half-length syllable in the *chastushki* tradition (see note 7 on p. 322) which provides a welcome rhythmic variety when the text is sung, as it was meant to be. The translation reproduces this hyper-metrical unstressed syllable in the respective positions: the third line of stanzas 3, 6, 8, 9 and 10.

7 Убёг is a colloquial variant of убежал (ran away).

8 The literal meaning of the second-person singular present form of шалить (to be naughty, to romp) is "you (singular) are being naughty", but it is used here as a one-word idiomatic expression indicating disagreement. Its meaning can be approximated as "this will not be allowed to happen".

9 The Russian language does not have a dedicated word for bats: they are called "flying mice" (летучие мыши). This presents a problem for adequate translation into Russian of the question "But do cats eat bats, I wonder?" which occurs to Alice during her fall. The solution found by Vysotsky is wonderfully symmetrical: flying mice – flying cats – flying dogs. Flying dogs actually exist (some of the giant species of bats are called so); only the middle part of this triplet is completely fantastic, an exercise in Carrollian zoology.

10 From the lyrics for the 1977 audio recording of *Alice in Wonderland* the musical. Vysotsky wrote over 30 songs for it and sang some of them in the performance.

The rhyme scheme of the original is *aaB'B' B'B'B'B' aa*. It is simplified to *aaBB CCCC aa* in the translation.

Олег Чухонцев

р. 1938

* * *

Н. Н. Вильмонту

Что там? Босой и сонный, выберусь из постели,
дверь распахнув, услышу, как на дворе светает:
это весенний гомон — на́ лето прилетели,
это осенний гогот — на зиму улетают.

Круг завершен, и снова боль моя так далёка,
что за седьмою далью кажется снова близкой,
и на равнине русской так же темна дорога,
как от стены Китайской и до стены берлинской.

Вот я опять вернулся, а ничего не понял.
Боль моя, неужели я ничего не значу,
а как последний олух всё позабыл, что помнил,
то ли смеюсь от горя, то ли от счастья плачу?

Бог мой, какая малость: скрипнула половица,
крикнул петух с нашеста, шлепнулась оземь капля.[1]
Это моя удача клювом ко мне стучится,
это с седьмого неба наземь спустилась цапля.

Вот уже песня в горле высохла, как чернила,
значит, другая повесть ждет своего сказанья.[2]
Снова тоска пространства птиц поднимает с Нила,
снова над полем брезжит призрачный дым скитанья...

Oleg Chukhontsev

b.1938

* * *

To N. N. Vilmont [3]

What's that? Unshod and sleepy, I will get up and out,[4]
hear an awoken yard that sunlight is creeping into:
this is a springtime hustle – flying in, summer-bound,
this is an autumn bustle – flying out for the winter.

Now, with the circle finished, my pain's once more so distant
that, round the cosmos yonder, it feels once more so near;
over the Russian flatlands, road darkness is as dismal
as from the Wall of China to the Berlin frontier.

See, though I keep returning, I'm none the wiser now.
Pain, tell me: am I really only a worthless trifle,
one, like a fool, forgetting things that he used to know?
Could it be grief I laugh from, could it be joy I cry for?

Goodness me, why so little? Creaks of a shaky floorboard,
crows of a morning rooster, splashes of raindrops heavy.
That is my luck beak-knocking, nudging me to step forward,
that is a heron getting down from the seventh heaven.

Song lines, like ink, have dried up inside my silent larynx,
so there must be another tale that awaits narration.
Once more the pull of vastness sends the Nile's birds a-flying,
once more the blurred horizon brims with peregrination...

ПОСЛЕВОЕННАЯ БАЛЛАДА

— Привезли листовое железо.
— Кто привез? — Да какой-то мужик.
— Кто такой? — А спроси живореза.[5]
— Сколько хочет? — Да бабу на штык.
— И хорош? — Хром на оба протеза.
А язык пулемет. Фронтовик.
— Да пошел!..

       — Привезли рубероид.
Изразцы привезли и горбыль.
— А не много? — Да щели прикроет.
Ты вдова, говорит, я бобыль. —
А глазищами так и буровит.[6]
— Ну-ка, дьявол, держись за костыль,
а не то...

       — Привезли черепицу.
— Убирайся! — Задаром отдам.
Разреши, говорит, притулиться
инвалиду ко вдовым ногам.
Я не евнух, и ты не девица,
ан поладим с грехом пополам.[7]

. . . .

Дом стоит. Черепица на крыше.
В доме печь: изразец к изразцу.
Кот на ходиках: слушайте, мыши.[8]
Сел малыш на колени к отцу.
А дымок над трубою всё выше,
выше, выше — и сказка к концу.

Ах, не ты ли — какими судьба́ми —
счастье русское? Как бы не так!
Сапоги оторва́ло с ногами.
Одиночество свищет в кулак.
И тоска моя рыщет ночами,
как собака, и воет во мрак.

Oleg Chukhontsev

A Post-War Ballad

– Metal sheets have arrived, never asked for.
– Who supplied them? – A chap of some sort.
– Who on earth might he be? – Ask the rascal.
– What's the price? – Why, a woman to court...
– Is he cute? – Wooden legs, pretty husky,
an ex-trooper, his tongue like a sword.
– Beat it!

        – There, lintels have been delivered,
patterned tiles and some beams for your home.
– Way too many. – No, I don't believe it.
You're a widow, he says, I'm alone,
with his eyes on her, ripping and cleaving.
– Hey you, devil on crutches, be gone!
Leave, or else...

        – Here's a stove for your kitchen.
– Go to hell! – Take for nothing, I beg.
Just permit me, a cripple, to edge in
for a place by a widow's real leg.
I'm no eunuch, and you are no virgin;
p'rhaps we will get along, what the heck.

. . . .

Here's a house with brand-new window lintels,
here's a stove, nothing more left to mend.
On a wall-clock a watchful cat lingers,[9]
and a kid sits on dad's knee, content.
As the smoke of the glimmering cinders
leaves the chimney, the tale has to end.

Could it be that it's you, – so evasive! –
Russian happiness? Never. Tough luck!
Boots and legs by a mine done away with,
loneliness makes the world come unstuck.
And my gloom every night wanders, wayward
like a dog, and it howls in the dark.

Notes

1 Нашест is a colloquial variant of the word насест (roost).

2 Here, сказанье is a gerund derived from the archaic verb сказывать (to narrate).

3 Nikolai Vilmont (1901–1986), a literary critic and translator from German.

4 The metrical scheme of this poem is –∪∪ –∪ –∪ ‖ –∪∪ –∪ –∪.

5 Живорез is an archaic word meaning a villain.

6 Here, буровить is a colloquial, and dialect, variation of the verb буравить (to drill), used in its figurative sense: to pierce with one's eyes.

7 Ан is used here as a conjunctive introducing a hypothetical scenario. The general function of this word is to indicate a frustrated expectation (either as a conjunctive or a colloquial particle).

8 Ходики is an old-fashioned word for a pendulum wall clock, usually with a decorated face.

9 This is a traditional decoration of the clock face. The cat often has moving eyes, driven by the clockwork.

Oleg Chukhontsev

Владимир Захаров

р. 1939

* * *

Здравствуй, матушка, костяная нога!
Что глядишь на меня с усмешкою?
Вижу я иль не вижу в тебе врага,
Но схожу я сегодня пешкою.[1]

Здравствуй, батюшка, несыто́й оскал![2]
Хорошо ль ты вчера накушался?[3]
Как ты звал меня, как рукой махал,
Но, как видишь, я не послушался.

На рассвете моя лишь утихнет злость,
Когда ветер свистит над рощею
В самодельный свисточек — пустую кость
Над неправдою нашей тощею.

Vladimir Zakharov

b.1939

* * *

Greetings, my fair Dame – Yagá Bony Leg! [4]
Why do you look at me ensnaringly?
Maybe I can't discern in your face a threat,
But today I'll be acting charily.

Greetings, my fair Sir – Never-Sated Fang! [5]
Did you feast at your pleasure yesterday?
Though you called me in, waving with your hand,
I am glad I did not say "yes" to you.

My resentment will only subside at dawn,
When the wind of the morning hours
Blows a crude home-made whistle – a hollow bone –
Over our untruth cadaverous.

Белые олеандры

Белые олеандры
Качаются, ах, качаются,
Ветер из пустыни
Не дает им просто цвести.
Прежние дни счастливые
Кончаются, ах, кончаются,
Солнца тяжелый шар
Стало трудно нести.

Белые олеандры
Перед стеною кирпичною,
Ветер из пустыни —
Это хор голосов:
«Встань, очнись и иди,
Брось заботы привычные,
Встань, очнись и иди —
Ангел сдвинет засов.

А на ушедшую жизнь
Оглянись без печали и гнева».
Мы погостили,
И нам пора по домам,
Белые олеандры
Под розовым небом Бер-Шевы,
Рядом с колодцем,
Из которого пил Авраам.

Vladimir Zakharov

The White Oleanders

The white oleanders
Are swaying, swaying.
The wind of the desert
Never leaves them alone.
The bliss on the chain of days
Is flaying, flaying.
The massive solar globe
Is harder to drag along.

The white oleanders
Set against bricks and mortar,
The wind of the desert –
A chorus that enunciates:
"Get up, come to, and go,
Abandon life's daily order.
Get up, come to, and go;
Angel, unbolt the gates.

As for your spent life,
Have neither sadness nor ire."
We've been on a visit,
And now it's time to go home.
White oleanders
Under Beersheba's pink sky,[6]
Next to a stone well
That Abraham used to drink from.

Notes

[1] This is a rare idiom based on the game of chess. It means "to tread carefully", "to proceed with caution".

[2] Несыто́й is an emotionally coloured colloquial variant of the rare adjective несы́тый (habitually hungry).

[3] Накушаться is a colloquial expression meaning to have eaten to excess (literally or figuratively, in the latter case often meaning to have been drinking to excess).

[4] Ба́ба Яга́ the Bony Leg is a witch from Slavic mythology. She is a complex character, with both positive and negative traits. Her bony leg has no rational explanation: it is just the way she is.

The rhythmic organisation of the original is quite complex and is closely linked to the meaning of the poem which combines the rational and mythological views of the world. The even lines (except line 8) follow the ∪∪– ∪∪– ∪–∪∪ pattern while the odd lines come in two shapes: ∪∪– ∪∪– ∪∪– ∪– (the rational theme) or ∪∪–∪∪ ∪∪–∪∪ (the mythological theme). The latter scheme is a simplification of what is known as the 5+5 folk-verse metre. It is based on a subtly modulated five-syllable foot where the compulsory stress in the middle is phrasal as well as lexical, with a secondary stress allowed on the first or the last syllable: ∪∪˝∪∪ or ´∪˝∪∪ or ∪∪˝∪´. A fine example of this metre is given by "Как за церковью, за немецкою..." by Pushkin who nearly succeeded in passing it for a genuine folk song ostensibly having been heard and recorded by him; he was found out 150 years later by Valentin Berestov (1928–1998). Here, this folk-verse metre occurs in lines 1 and 5, where the fantastic characters are introduced; lines 7–8 are also written in it. After that the rational theme (first introduced in line 3) takes over.

The translation closely approximates the rhythmic scheme of the original but makes no attempt to reproduce the folk verse foot which does not have the required associations in English anyway.

[5] A reference to the Grey Wolf of Russian folk tales.

[6] Beersheba is a town in the Negev desert in Israel.

Иосиф Бродский

1940—1996

Шесть лет спустя

Так долго вместе прожили, что вновь
второе января пришлось на вторник,
что удивленно поднятая бровь,
как со стекла автомобиля — дворник,
    с лица сгоняла смутную печаль,
    незамутненной оставляя даль.

Так долго вместе прожили, что снег
коль выпадал, то думалось — навеки,
что, дабы не зажмуривать ей век,
я прикрывал ладонью их, и веки,
    не веря, что их пробуют спасти,
    метались там, как бабочки в горсти.

Так чужды были всякой новизне,
что тесные объятия во сне
    бесчестили любой психоанализ;
что губы, припадавшие к плечу,
с моими, задувавшими свечу,
    не видя дел иных, соединялись.

Так долго вместе прожили, что роз
семейство на обшарпанных обоях
сменилось целой рощею берез,
и деньги появились у обоих,
    и тридцать дней над морем, языкат,
    грозил пожаром Турции закат.

Так долго вместе прожили без книг,
без мебели, без утвари на старом
диванчике, что — прежде, чем возник, —

Joseph Brodsky

1940–1996

SIX YEARS SINCE [1]

We'd lived together for so long that twice
the year's day two had fallen on a Tuesday;
that, when her eyebrow lifted in surprise,
it swept off, like screen wipers on a bruised day,
  her face's vague expression of her blues,
  while making plain to see the forward views.

We'd lived together for so long that snows
were falling, when they fell, as if forever;
that, to prevent her eyes being forced to close,
I'd reach for them and use my hand for cover,
  and her eyelids, as if they disagreed,
  would jolt, like butterflies inside a grip.

We had been so blasé of every craze
that in our sleep we'd share a tight embrace,
  thus bringing Freud's whole method into scandal;
that when her lips towards my arm inclined
without a purpose, they my lips would find,
  as mine were busy blowing out the candle.

We'd lived together for so long, the mauve
of roses on wallpaper barely hanging
had turned into the green of a birch grove;
then finally we both came into money.
  For thirty days the Turkish coast received
  The tongues of sunset stretched across the sea. [2]

We'd lived together for so long without
books, crockery or furniture (a plank bed
was it) that the triangle looked – no doubt –

Laureate of the Nobel Prize in Literature: 1987, "for an all-embracing authorship, imbued with clarity of thought and poetic intensity".

был треугольник перпендикуляром,
   восставленным знакомыми стойма [3]
   над слившимися точками двумя.

Так долго вместе прожили мы с ней,
что сделали из собственных теней
   мы дверь себе — работаешь ли, спишь ли,
но створки не распахивались врозь,
и мы прошли их, видимо, насквозь
   и черным ходом в будущее вышли.

1968

initially more like a line and plummet
    suspended by some mutual friends above
    two points, fused into one by half and half.

We'd lived together for so long, we'd made
a two-leaved door from our own shadows splayed
    and oftentimes behind it worked or rested.
Since either leaf refused to swing alone,
It was the *two* of us who left their home
    and into future's back door made their exit.

1968

Итака

Воротиться сюда через двадцать лет,
отыскать в песке босиком свой след.
И поднимет барбос лай на весь причал
не признаться, что рад, а что одичал.

Хочешь, скинь с себя пропотевший хлам;
но прислуга мертва опознать твой шрам.
А одну, что тебя, говорят, ждала,
не найти нигде, ибо всем дала.

Твой пацан подрос; он и сам матрос,
и глядит на тебя, точно ты — отброс.
И язык, на котором вокруг орут,
разбирать, похоже, напрасный труд.

То ли остров не тот, то ли впрямь, залив⁴
синевой зрачок, стал твой глаз брезглив:
От куска земли горизонт волна
не забудет, видать, набегая на.⁵

1993

ULYSSES [6]

To return to this place after twenty suns,
to the print of your foot in the seaside sand.
Seeing you on the quay, your old dog will bark
not for joy, but to say he's free as a lark.

You may take off your rags, marked and sweat-suffused,
but the nurse is dead and your scar no use.
And the only one, who, they said, would wait
for your coming back, by all men gets laid.

Your wee lad is a man guzzling sailors' rum,
looking down at you, as if you were scum.
It's a waste of time trying to make out
the new language, in which folks around you shout.

Is this not your isle? Has your cornea, tinged
with the navy blue, got fastidious?
True enough, a wave can't forget skylines
just because on a scrap of dry earth it lands.

1993

Notes

[1] The form of this poem is discussed on p. xlv.

[2] They are holidaying on the Crimean shore of the Black Sea, opposite Turkey. Turkish resorts, so popular with Russian holidaymakers these days, were unreachable for them at the time.

[3] Восставить is a rare verb which occurs almost exclusively as part of the mathematical term "восставить перпендикуляр" (to raise a perpendicular). It is used here as part of an extended geometric metaphor triggered by the implied expression "love triangle".

[4] The word залив may initially be perceived here as a noun, meaning a bay or a shallow creek, because of the presence of the word остров (island) in the same position within a grammatically similar structure earlier in the line. However, the following line reveals that залив is actually an adverbial participle, meaning "having filled up", "having flooded" or "having covered [with liquid]". The utilisation of this homonymy, in combination with Brodsky's signature enjambment, is likely to be a ploy intended to emphasise the theme of frustrated expectations.

[5] Brodsky violates Russian grammar here, using an English-style construct. Similar things are also happening earlier in the poem (e.g. in line 4), although they are less obvious. This could be interpreted as an indication that Ulysses' problem with the language of the locals is mutual.

[6] In the original the title is 'Ithaca', the home island of Ulysses. Brodsky's Ithaca is St Petersburg, except that he never returned there. A 20-years absence, the dog, the beggars' rags (used as a disguise), the old nurse and a distinctive scar all feature in Homer's *Odyssey*.

The metre of the original is a 4-beat *dolnik* leaning towards a logaoedic: ∪∪– ∪(∪) – ‖ ∪∪– ∪–. The only variation allowed by this scheme is used extensively, with approximately half of the lines containing the optional syllable in the second foot, so the overall metrical feel is that of *dolnik*. The caesura is shifted to the right in lines 11–12 that comment on the language change.

Дмитрий А. Пригов

1940—2007

Письмо из древней Греции древнеяпонскому другу

А что в Японии, по-прежнему ль Фудзи́
Колышется словно на бедрах ткань косая
По-прежнему ли ласточки с Янцзы
Слетаются на праздник Хоккусая

По-прежнему ли Ямомото-сан
Любуется на ширмы из Киото
И кисточкой проводит по усам
Когда его по-женски кликнет кто-то

По-прежнему ли в дикой Русь-земле
Живут не окрестясь антропофаги
Но умные и пишут на бумаге
И, говорят, слыхали обо мне

Dmitri A. Prigov

1940–2007

AN ANCIENT GREEK'S LETTER
TO HIS ANCIENT-JAPANESE FRIEND

How is Nippon these days: does Fuji-san
still sway like waistband fabric on a geisha?
Do swifts that nest by the Yangtze still come
for annual Hokusai-fest celebrations?

Does most respected Nakamura still [1]
admire the folding screens from Aomori,
and feather his moustache with gentle skill
whenever he can hear a lady calling?

And is the savage land that they call Rus
still peopled by profane anthropophages,
though clever ones, who scribe on paper pages,
and who reportedly have heard of us?

КУЛИКОВО

Вот всех я по местам расставил
Вот этих справа я поставил
Вот этих слева я поставил
Всех прочих на потом оставил
Поляков на потом оставил
Французов на потом оставил
И немцев на потом оставил
Вот ангелов своих наставил
И сверху воронов поставил
И прочих птиц вверху поставил
А снизу поле предоставил
Для битвы поле предоставил
Его деревьями уставил
Дубами-елями уставил
Кустами кое-где обставил
Травою мягкой застелил
Букашкой мелкой населил
Пусть будет всё, как я представил
Пусть все живут, как я заставил
Пусть все умрут, как я заставил

Так победят сегодня русские
Ведь неплохие парни русские
И девки неплохие русские
Они страдали много, русские
Терпели ужасы нерусские
Так победят сегодня русские

Что будет здесь, коль уж сейчас
Земля крошится уж сейчас
И небо пыльно уж сейчас
Породы рушатся подземные
И воды мечутся подземные
И твари мечутся подземные
И люди бегают наземные
Туда-сюда бегут приземные
И птицы поднялись надземные
Все птицы-вороны надземные

Kulikóvo [2]

I've set both parties right in place and
These people – on the right I placed and
Those people – on the left I placed and
I've left all others off for later
I left the Polacks off for later
I left the Frenchies off for later
I left the Germans off for later [3]
I've made my angels keep an eye there
I've made the ravens overfly them
And other birdies overfly them
And down below, a field I've laid them
A battlefield below I've laid them
With trees in places overlaying
With oak-trees, fir-trees overlaying
With moss and mushrooms underlaying
I covered all by green grass rugs
And populated with small bugs
May all be just as I have sighted
May each one live as I decided
May each one die as I decided

Today the winners shall be Russians
Indeed they are good guys, those Russians
And they have lovely girls, those Russians
They've suffered quite a lot, poor Russians
Some grave atrocities un-Russian
Today the victory be Russian

What will ensue when at this time
The earth is crumbling, at this time
The air is dusty at this time
While ores are crushing underground
And waters rushing underground
And beasties rushing underground
And folks are running overground
So fast and near to the ground
And birds have lifted off the ground
All fliers-ravens – off the ground

А всё ж татары поприятней
И имена их поприятней
И голоса их поприятней
Да и повадка поприятней
Хоть русские и поопрятней
А всё ж татары поприятней
Так пусть татары победят
Отсюда всё мне будет видно
Татары, значит, победят
А впрочем — завтра будет видно

And yet the Tartars are the nicer
Their given names appear the nicer
Their voices, too, appear the nicer
Their manners also seem the nicer
The Russians may well be the nattier
And yet the Tartars are the nicer
The Tartars hence deserve to win
From here the battle I will see
Indeed, the Tartars are to win
Although... tomorrow I shall see

Notes

[1] It is Yamomoto [*sic*] in the original. The character is completely fantastic, as are some other details in the poem, so the translation uses a common Japanese surname to avoid an unintended association with Admiral Isoroku Yamamoto. There is no such problem in the original, as Admiral Yamamoto is not widely known in Russia (even though he started his career during the Russo-Japanese war).

[2] On the field of Kulikovo, in 1380, Russian armies defeated the Tartars (the name by which the diverse tribes of the Golden Horde are traditionally identified) in what was probably the largest medieval battle in Europe. This event traditionally marks the beginning of the decline of the Golden Horde rule of Russia, although the historic reality is more complex.

The identical and nearly-identical rhymes are a feature of the original: see the discussion on p. xxxiv.

[3] The references are to the 17th-century Polish invasion, Napoleonic invasion of 1812 and World War II.

Виктор Кривулин

1944—2001

Арфа с ирландского пенни

оставили земли — но книги заселим
оставленной родиной речью напевной
или нереальна ирландская зелень
и рыжая прядка травы патрике́вны [1]

и смутная арфа с потертого пенни
в пустой ленинград занесенная кем-то
из реэмигрантов — и хриплое пенье
когда его брали, врага и агента

Victor Krivulin

1944–2001

THE HARP ON AN IRISH COIN

we've left native lands – but will populate verses
with birth-country soil and its parlance entrancing
or is it unreal: the profuse irish verdure
along with the gingery locks of our grasses

and also the harp half-effaced on a shilling [2]
once into bare leningrad brought by an ageing
returning ex-pat – and the sounds of hoarse singing
when they came to take him, an enemy agent

ЯПОНСКИЙ ПЕРЕВОДЧИК

я был наверное тем самым
японцем что явился людям
с переведенным дурно мандельштамом
но русскому суду за это неподсуден

пускай меня возьмут на суд китайский
пускай позорную повяжут мне повязку
пускай посодят связанным в повозку [3]
и возят по стране пока я не покаюсь

что не проник ему ни прямо в душу
ни по касательной, что никаким шицзи́ном
не поверял строки с притихшим керосином
что сторублевок жертвенных не жег
на примусе пред Господом единым

поэт зашитый в кожаный мешок
подвешенный к ветвям цветущей груши —
он тоже соловей
хоть слушай хоть не слушай

2000

Japanese Translator [4]

i must have been that quite audacious
son of japan appearing to the people
with mandelstám in woeful mistranslation [5]
but this in russia would not be illegal

may i be tried under the laws of china
may i be forced a shameful band to wear
may i be bound and driven everywhere
till i confess that i have failed the challenge

in that his soul did not direct my flair
at all; that i could not use the shi jing well [6]
to validate the line about the kerosene smell [7]
nor did i burn my roubles on the rack
atop a primus stove for the Redeemer [8]

a poet sewn into a leather sack
that hangs from branches of a blooming pear – [9]
he is a songbird too
whether or not you care

2000

Notes

[1] "Трава Патрикевна" is based on "Лиса Патрикевна", the fox of Russian folk tales. Her nickname is actually a patronymic derived from the name Патрикей, the Russian variant of Patrick. St Patrick (св. Патрикей) is venerated in the Orthodox Church too, as he was canonised before the East-West schism. At the same time, this line expressly refers to red hair, an Irish trait. So both the name of the fox and the colour of its fur reinforce the parallel between the two emigrations.

[2] It is a penny rather than a shilling in the original. See the discussion of this substitution on p. xlv.

[3] Посодят is a corrupt form of the verb посадят, which can be used colloquially to disambiguate the intended secondary meaning (they will imprison) from the main meaning (they will sit [somebody] down / they will offer a seat). Note also the sonority with позорную (shameful; singular accusative feminine form) of the previous line.

[4] The unusual rhyme scheme of the original (*ABAB CDDC EFFgF gExE*) is reproduced in the translation.

[5] A reference to a poem by Osip Mandelstam:

> Татары, узбеки и ненцы,
> И весь украинский народ,
> И даже приволжские немцы
> К себе переводчиков ждут.
>
> И, может быть, в эту минуту
> Меня на турецкий язык
> Японец какой переводит
> И прямо мне в душу проник.
>
> •
>
> The Tatars, the Nenets, the Georgians,
> And every Ukrainian, too,
> And even "das Volk" – Volga Germans
> Invite other folks to translate.
>
> It could be that right at this moment
> A son of Japan starts to scrawl
> My poem translated to Turkish,
> His flair coming straight from my soul.

⁶ *Shi Jing*, or *Shih Ching* (*Book of Odes*, or *Classics of Poetry*) is an influential collection of ancient Chinese poetry. Compilation of this canon is traditionally credited to Confucius (551–479 BC).

⁷ A reference to the following poem by Mandelstam:

> Мы с тобой на кухне посидим,
> Сладко пахнет белый керосин.
>
> Острый нож да хлеба каравай...
> Хочешь, примус туго накачай.
>
> А не то веревок собери
> Завязать корзину до зари,
>
> Чтобы нам уехать на вокзал,
> Где бы нас никто не отыскал.
>
> •
>
> In the kitchen sat, we will stay in.
> The sweet odour of white kerosene.
>
> There's a knife beside a round bread loaf...
> If you wish, pump up the primus stove.
>
> Otherwise go glean assorted strings:
> At first light we need to pack our things,
>
> Reach the station whereat train meets train,
> So that all may look for us in vain.

⁸ Krivulin means the Chinese ritual of burning "ghost money" in veneration of one's departed ancestors. The image is deliberately mixed culturally, with references to the Russian currency and Christianity.

⁹ A blooming pear appears in yet another poem by Mandelstam, but it is unlikely that Krivulin is referring to it here.

The one who wakes

проснувшийся

Алексей Цветков

р. 1947

* * *

Я мечтал подружиться с совой, но увы,
Никогда я на воле не видел совы,
Не сходя с городской карусели.
И хоть память моя оплыла, как свеча,
Я запомнил, что ходики в виде сыча [1]
Над столом моим в детстве висели.

Я пытался мышам навязаться в друзья,
Я к ним в гости, как равный, ходил без ружья,
Но хозяева были в отъезде,
И когда я в ангине лежал, не дыша,
Мне совали в постель надувного мыша [2]
Со свистком в неожиданном месте.

Я ходил в зоопарк посмотреть на зверей,
Застывал истуканом у дачных дверей,
Где сороки в потемках трещали,
Но из летнего леса мне хмурилась вновь
Деревянная жизнь, порошковая кровь,
Бесполезная дружба с вещами.

Отвинчу я усталую голову прочь,
Побросаю колесики в дачную ночь
И свистульку из задницы выну,
Чтоб шептали мне мыши живые слова,
Чтоб военную песню мне пела сова,
Как большому, но глупому сыну.

Alexei Tsvetkov

Alexei Tsvetkov

b.1947

* * *

I have dreamed of befriending an owl, but alas!
In my life I have never seen one flying past
From the city life merry-go-round.
Though my memory gutters like candles ablaze,
I remember the pendulum timepiece owl-faced,
Over my childhood desk looking out.

I have tried to impose friendship on local mice,
Pay a visit unarmed, as if I were their size,
But the hosts were not in to receive it.
And when I couldn't breathe for my throat sore and red,
Then a squeezable mouse was thrust into my bed
With a whistle in... who would believe it.

I would visit a zoo to observe a wild boar,
I would pause by the summer log-cabin front door,
Hearing magpies' night-time noisy chatting.
But the woodlands would frown at this peering young lad
With non-sentient life and its surrogate blood,
All those pointless inanimate chum-things.

I'll unscrew the exhausted old noggin outright,
I will throw all the cogs to the log-cabin night,
Have the whistle removed from my rear –
So that mice may come whispering live before long,
And an owl may intone me an old battle song [3]
As his grown-up but asinine heir.

We must disclaim any relationship between the style of these trans-
lations and that of Alexei Tsvetkov's original English-language poetry.
We are grateful to Dr Tsvetkov, who gave us the permission to include
his entry in the anthology even though he disagrees with our approach
to translation.

* * *

отверни гидрант и вода тверда
ни умыть лица ни набрать ведра
и насос перегрыз ремни
затупился лом не берет кирка
потому что как смерть вода крепка
хоть совсем ее отмени

все события в ней отразились врозь
хоть рояль на соседа с балкона сбрось
он как новенький невредим
и язык во рту нестерпимо бел
видно пили мы разведенный мел
а теперь его так едим

бесполезный звук из воды возник
не проходит воздух в глухой тростник
захлебнулась твоя свирель
прозвенит гранит по краям ведра
но в замерзшем времени нет вреда
для растений звезд и зверей

потому что слеп известковый мозг
потому что мир это горный воск
застывающий без труда
и в колодезном круге верней чем ты
навсегда отразила его черты
эта каменная вода

Alexei Tsvetkov

* * *

turn the well-pump tap and the water's stuck
cannot wash my face cannot fill a tank
and the pump has chewed through the belt
the crowbar's gone blunt tried the pick no diff
since like death the water is rigid stiff
you might cancel it just as well

see events in it in a severed state
if a piano you were to defenestrate
on a neighbor they'd look like new
in your mouth the festering tongue is bleached
did we drink diluted fine chalk and switched
then to chalk that we were to chew

all the water makes is a useless zap
since the air is trapped in the reed clogged up
so your flute can do naught but hiss [4]
pebbles fill the tank as its rim they ram
but in frozen time there can not be harm
not for plants or planets or beasts

since the lime brain must be bereft of sight
since the whole wide world is ozokerite [5]
it can stiffen and does so fast
in the wellhead ring faithful more than you
an eternal depiction of this milieu
is displayed by the water crust

Notes

[1] See note 8 on p. 256.

[2] The correct Russian word for mouse is мышь (feminine). The word мыш does not officially exist but can be used colloquially for a humorous reference to a male mouse.

[3] An apparent reference to the poem 'Снигирь' (Bullfinch) by Gavriil Derzhavin (1743–1816). It was written on the death of a famous Russian general and begins with the lines

> Что ты заводишь песню военну
> Флейте подобно, милый снигирь?
>
> •
>
> Why are you starting a battle song now,
> As would a flutist, bullfinch my dear?

The modern spelling of the words военну and снигирь is военную (military; adjective, singular accusative feminine form) and снегирь (bullfinch).

[4] A possible reference to the following poem by Osip Mandelstam:

> Есть иволги в лесах, и гласных долгота
> В тонических стихах единственная мера,
> Но только раз в году бывает разлита́
> В природе длительность, как в метрике Гомера.
>
> Как бы цезурою зияет этот день:
> Уже с утра покой и трудные длинноты,
> Волы на пастбище, и золотая лень
> Из тростника извлечь богатство целой ноты.
>
> •
>
> Yes, there are orioles, and vowels sounding slow
> In classic verse where they act as the rhythm conductor;
> But only once a year all nature overflows
> With languid lengthiness, like quantitative dactyls.
>
> Caesura-gaping are those annual climax days:
> Right from the start a rest, and then *continuo* tricksome,
> The oxen graze away; and it's a golden laze
> To take a whole note's wealth out of a hollow reed stem.

[5] Ozokerite is a mineral paraffin resembling bee wax and found in mountainous areas (the Russian name is literally "mountain wax").

Иван Жданов

р. 1948

* * *

Я не лунатик, я ногами сплю.
Вокруг меня помпезные колонны —
я их корней не чувствую, они —
застывшие глотки́ незримых горл.
Что недопито или что еще
им выпить предстоит, какой отравы?
Учитывая почвы этих мест,
они должны быть красными, как кровь.
Но нет, в подтеках, серые, на них
надёван камень, но не лунной пробы,[1]
а той, что близок звук какой-то — «у».
Вот доигрался, вот уже собаки
хватают сумрак заполошным лаем,[2]
как одеяло, под которым чуют
клубящийся волчатник или след.[3]
След? Но кому он нужен, этот след?
Пусть кто-нибудь его другой доносит.
А я стою. Вокруг меня колонны —
Бирнамский лес, застывший на ходу.

Ivan Zhdanov

b.1948

* * *

Not a somnambulist's, my sleep is with my feet.
I am surrounded by tall, pompous columns
whose roots I am not sensing, those are just
suspended gulps of throats that can't be seen.
What have they not drunk up yet and what else
are they to drink in future, what's their poison?
Considering our parts' prevailing soil,
The columns ought to show the very hue
of blood, but they are runny grey; and dressed
in stone, which is not of the moonstone standard,
but rather like a sound, perhaps it's "w".
See what I've done: already dogs are tearing
by endless strident bark the setting darkness
like a duvet, under which they are sensing
the whirlwind of wolf cubs or someone's trail.
A trail? But who would ever need this trail?
Let it be one behind another person.
I'm standing still, surrounded by the columns:
Great Birnam wood that froze between its steps.

* * *

Запомнил я цветные сны шмеля:
плыла сквозь них ко мне моя земля.

Но неба для нее не подобрать —
пуста моя открытая тетрадь.

Так тучи пробегают по лицу,
так небо приближается к концу.

Оно уже дописано во мне,
оставьте меня с ним наедине.

* * *

I still recall a bumble bee's bright dreams:
through them my land toward me used to drift.

But where to find a sky that it will match?
My open notepad hasn't yet been touched.

Thus stormy clouds across one's forehead flit,
thus will the sky its consummation meet.

It is inside me finished up at last,
and now would you excuse the two of us.

Notes

[1] Надёван is the short form of the colloquial participle надёванный derived from the verb надевать (to put on). The corresponding normative participle is надетый (full form), надет (short form).

[2] Заполошный is a rare adjective related to the word переполох (commotion).

[3] Here, волчатник means a litter of wolf cubs.

Михаил Айзенберг

р. 1948

* * *

Вот последнее: каждый порез на счету.
И обуженный воздух идет в высоту,
каждой тенью себя повторяет.

Вот кора в узелках, и стена проросла.
Потревоженной молью ныряет зола,
и не скажешь, как память ныряет.

Тем и жить, наконец, просчитав на шаги
всё, что возле и вровень послушной рутине.

Я привязанный камень. Всё у́же круги.

Так прижмись к середине, прижмись к середине.

1975

Mikhail Aizenberg

b.1948

* * *

Here's the last: all the cuts will add up to a score;
air forced out into narrowing spaces will soar,
in each shadow beneath it self-miming.

Here is bark raked with bumps, and a wall growing mould.
See the ashes nose-dive like a shooed-away moth,
and there's nothing like memory diving.

Should I try to live thus, having measured at last
all that's near and which levels with tame daily twiddle?

I'm a stone on a string, making narrowing laps.

So you cling to the middle, you cling to the middle.[1]

1975

* * *

Грубые вещи со мной роднятся,
наше братанье не за горами.
Если не знаешь, на что равняться —
вон их команда пошла дворами.

Хохот и свист в проходном подъезде.
Новый пролом вековой ограды.
Раз не уходишь, стоишь на месте,
вроде как свой. А своим мы рады.

Я от своих ухожу лет сто уж.
Выхода жду на пути обратном,
чтобы сказать им: хоть я и сторож,
грубые вещи, но я не брат вам.[2]

* * *

Impudent things try to claim my kinship,
fraternisation is in the offing.
If you're confused, if your life's a clean sheet,
look: there's a gang of them coming over.

Cat-calls and hoots in the street abound.
Breakage: a gap in our age-old railing.
Since you won't leave, since you stick around,
you're like our kin, so with joy we hail you.

I've left behind scores of kindred people;
These will be there when I'm back, I gather.
So I will tell them: though I'm the keeper,
impudent things, I am not your brother.

Notes

[1] Steadily shortening stanzas support the image of a shortening string.

[2] A turned around quotation from Gen. 4: 9 ("разве я сторож брату моему?", "Am I my brother's keeper?").

Бахыт Кенжеев

р. 1950

* * *

Сердце хитрит — ни во что оно толком не верит.
Бьется, болеет, плутает по скользким дорогам,
плачет взахлеб — и отчета не держит ни перед
кем, разве только по смерти, пред Господом Богом.

Слушай, шепчу ему, в медленном воздухе этом
я постараюсь напиться пронзительным светом,
вязом и мрамором стану, отчаюсь, увяну,
солью аттической сдобрю смердящую рану.

Разве не видишь, не чувствуешь — солнце садится,
в сторону дома летит узкогрудая птица,
разве не слышишь — писец на пергаменте новом
что-то со скрипом выводит пером тростниковым?

Вот и натешилось. Сколько свободы и горя!
Словно скитаний и горечи в Ветхом Завете.
Реки торопятся к морю — но синему морю
не переполниться — и возвращается ветер,

и возвращается дождь, и военная лютня
всё отдаленней играет, и всё бесприютней,
и фонарей, фонарей бесконечная лента...
Что они строятся — или прощаются с кем-то?

Bakhyt Kenjeev

b.1950

* * *

I say my heart's being a cheat, not a proper believer.
Jolting and pining, it strays onto slippery slopes,
cries itself out and reports to not one of the living,
only perhaps after death, to the Lord of the Hosts.

Listen, I whisper to it: in this languorous air
I'll try to quench all my thirst with that piercing bright glare,
I'll be an elm-tree and marble – dispirited, wizen,
with Attic salt I'll relieve a malodorous lesion.

Surely you *can* see and sense that the sun is declining,
and that a slim-chested bird is aloft, homeward flying?
surely you *can* hear a scribe on a fresh piece of vellum
write with a creaky reed pen the first lines of a volume?

Happier now, having had so much freedom and dolour
that it would match the Old Testament's roving and rancour?
Rivers run into the sea, yet the sea won't be fuller.
Whirling about in his circuits, the wind comes around,[1]

so once again does the rain, with a marching-band flutist
sounding increasingly distant, increasingly rootless.
Lampposts, those lampposts in ranks stretching to the horizon...
Why are they lining up? May they be bidding good-bye there?

* * *

Плещет вода несвежая в бурдюке.
Выбраться бы и мне, наконец, к реке
или колодцу, что ли, но карте ветхой
лучше не верить. Двигаются пески,
веку прошедшему не протянуть руки,
сердцу — не тяготиться грудною клеткой.

На спину ляжешь, посмотришь наверх — а там
та же безгласность, по тем же кружат местам
звезды немытые. Холодно, дивно, грустно.
В наших краях, где смертелен напор времен,
всадник не верит, что сгинет в пустыне он.
Падает беркут, потоки меняют русло.

Выйти к жилью, переподковать коня
с мордой усталой. Должно быть, не для меня
из-за наследства грызня на далекой тризне
по золотому, черному. Пронеслась
и просверкала. Не мучайся. Даже князь
тьмы, вероятно, не ведает смысла жизни.

* * *

Splashes of water, stale, in a saddlebag.[2]
It'd help to reach, finally, a river bank,
or perhaps a well, but a map of this vintage
isn't trustworthy. The sand dunes shift,
your arm won't stretch over the century rift
nor will your heart feel burdened by its rib cage.

Lie on your back, take a glance at the sky – but there
is the same voicelessness turning the same old sphere,
planets unwashed. It is cold; it is wondrous, doleful.
He who rides here, where Time passes in deadly haste,
would not believe he's to vanish there in the waste.
Eagles make stoops, a new course by a stream is followed.

Here is a dwelling, a place to reshoe the steed,
his face looking tired. Against my creed
would be an inheritance brawl at the mourning
for the gold and the black. She's pranced
and glittered away. Stop wondering. Even the Prince
of Darkness isn't likely cognisant of Life's meaning.[3]

Notes

---

[1] The slight liberty taken with the quotation from Eccles. 1: 6–7, including changing the order of images, reflects the way this quotation is handled in the original.

[2] The general metre of the original is $-\cup\cup\ -\cup\cup\ -\cup\cup\ -\cup\ -(\cup)$, although there are many minor deviations from it: only the second stanza is 100% compliant with this scheme. Unusually, the majority of deviations are concentrated in the beginning of the piece (the regular pattern does not appear in full until line 5), so the rhythm wanders a little until the sight of the night sky sets things straight. The translation approximates this quality by rendering the first and the last stanzas in accentual verse while reproducing the exact logaoedic metre of the second stanza.

The nomadic motif is typical of Kenjeev, despite the fact that he left Kazakhstan as a young boy and does not even speak the language. He is published there, both in the original Russian and in Kazakh translation.

[3] The chain of enjambments in the last stanza is a feature of the original.

Александр Еременко

р. 1950

Сонет без рифм

Мы говорим на разных языках.
Ты бесишься, как маленькая лошадь,
а я стою в траве перед веревкой
и не могу развесить мой сонет.

Он падает, а я его ловлю.
Давай простим друг друга для начала,
развяжем этот узел немудреный
и свяжем новый, на другой манер.

Но так, чтобы друг друга не задеть,
не потревожить руку или ногу,
не перерезать глотку, наконец.

Чтоб каждый, кто летает и летит,
по воздуху по этому летая,
летел бы дальше, сколько ему влезет.

Alexander Yeryomenko

b.1950

AN UNRHYMED SONNET [1]

It is as if we spoke in different tongues.
You thrash about, much like a little mare,
while I stand on the lawn before a clothes line
and cannot hang my sonnet out to dry.

It's falling, and I catch it as it falls.
To start with, let us pardon one another;
let us untie this knot uncomplicated
and tie a new one in a different way.

But only such that neither one is hurt,
not to discomfort arms or legs or something
and not to cut a throat at any rate.

So that each one who flies and who's in flight,
who's flying right across this very air
could fly and fly as long as he may fancy.

* * *

Человек похож на термопару:
если слева чуточку нагреть,
развернется справа для удара.
Дальше не положено смотреть.

Даже если всё переиначить —
то нагнется к твоему плечу
в позе, приспособленной для плача…
Дальше тоже видеть не хочу.

* * *

Human beings resemble thermocouples.[2]
If you warm a specimen's left side,
it will swing its shoulder, arm and knuckles,
and the rest is a forbidden sight. ·

Try this under modified conditions,
it will drop its head onto your chest
to assume the lachrymose position;
equally I wouldn't watch the rest.

Notes

[1] From the cycle 'Невенок сонетов' (A Non-Crown of Sonnets). Despite being unrhymed, this poem exhibits several features of a sonnet, including an iambic metre, the stanzaic form and the presence of a *volta*. Other sonnets in the cycle are rhymed, some of them in extreme ways.

[2] Yeremenko has a penchant for technological jargon and uses it very skilfully. However, in this poem he is evidently mistaken: the image is of a bimetal thermal switch, not a thermocouple. While the two devices have similar constructions, only the former bends one way or another when it is heated or cooled. The latter produces a weak electric current instead.

Alexander Yeryomenko

Сергей Гандлевский

р. 1952

* * *

всё разом — вещи в коридоре
отъезд и сборы впопыхах
шесть вялых роз и крематорий
и предсказание в стихах
другие сборы путь не близок
себя в трюмо а у трюмо
засохший яблока огрызок
се одиночество само [1]
или короткою порою
десятилетие назад
она и он как брат с сестрою
друг другу что-то говорят
обоев клетку голубую
и обязательный хрусталь
семейных праздников любую
подробность каждую деталь
включая освещенье комнат
и мебель тумбочку комод
и лыжи за комодом — вспомнит
проснувшийся и вновь заснет

Sergey Gandlevsky

b.1952

* * *

at once: things piled up in the doorway
departure and being out of time
limp roses and the crematorium
and in one's verse a mantic line
another trip a longer journey
one's mirror gazing from the shelf
the dried unfinished apple on it
(behold that's loneliness itself)
or in the briefest of the seasons
ten anniversaries ago
her talking to him like a sibling
and him to her replying so
the old wallpaper in abrasions
the mandatory champagne flutes
all the familial celebrations
each little detail each minúte
speck on the floorboards in the hallway
the wardrobe jammed into the cove
the skis behind it – all recalled by
the one who wakes and dozes off

На смерть И. Б.

Здесь когда-то ты жила, старшеклассницей была,
А сравнительно недавно своевольно умерла.
Как, наверное, должна скверно тикать тишина,
Если женщине-красавице жизнь стала не мила.
Уроженец здешних мест, средних лет, таков, как есть,
Ради холода спинного навещаю твой подъезд.
Что ли роз на все возьму, на кладбище отвезу,
Уроню, как это водится, нетрезвую слезу...
Я ль не лез в окно к тебе из ревности, по злобе́
По гремучей водосточной к небу задранной трубе?
Хорошо быть молодым, молодым и пьяным в дым —
Четверть века, четверть века зряшным подвигам моим!
Голосом, разрезом глаз с толку сбит в толпе не раз,
Я всегда обознавался, не ошибся лишь сейчас,
Не ослышался — мертва. Пошла кругом голова.
Не любила меня отроду, но ты была жива.

Кто б на ножки поднялся́, в дно головкой уперся́,
Поднатужился, чтоб разом смерть была, да вышла вся!
Воскресать так воскресать! Встали в рост отец и мать.
Друг Сопровский оживает, подбивает выпивать.
Мы «андроповки» берем, что-то первая коло́м —
Комом в горле, слуцким слогом да частушечным стихом.
Так от радости пьяны, гибелью опалены,
В черно-белой кинохронике вертаются с войны.[2]
Нарастает стук колес, и душа идет вразнос.
На вокзале марш играют — слепнет музыка от слез.
Вот и ты — одна из них. Мельком видишь нас двоих,
Кратко на фиг посылаешь обожателей своих.
Вижу я сквозь толчею тебя прежнюю, ничью,
Уходящую безмолвно прямо в молодость твою.
Ну, иди себе, иди. Все плохое позади.
И отныне, надо думать, хорошее впереди.
Как в былые времена, встань у школьного окна.
Имя, девичью фамилию выговорит тишина.

1998

ON THE DEATH OF I.B.[3]

Here a long time back you dwelt, to a local high school went,
And you recently decided – willfully – your life to end.
Horrid it must be to yield to a clock's soliloquy
If a woman so damn beautiful should favor to not be.
Born and bred right in these parts, middle aged, sincere at heart,
For the sake of goosebump rushes I keep walking past your flat.
Should I buy some roses dear, take them to the grave austere
Where I might as well conventionally shed a drunken tear?
Once an angry jealous guy, didn't I in your window dive
Having scaled a hard and rattling drainpipe towering sky-high?
It feels good when you are young and unconscionably drunk;
It's been nigh a quarter century since that unfruitful stunt.
When in public, more than once I've misrecognized your stance,
Got confused by voice resemblance... not this time, though – not a chance.
It has been confirmed: you died. Suddenly my head is light.
True, you never ever loved me, but at least you were alive.

Who would stand up on his toes, stretch himself and say "Here goes!"
Throwing Death out of the casket with a bunch of heavy blows?[4]
And as he pulls off the trick, back to life my parents spring.
Now my friend Sopróvsky's breathing, offering to have a drink.[5]
Once Andrópovka is bought, the first shot sticks in the throat[6]
As a lump of hoarse folk couplets interlaced with Slutsky's throb.[7]
This is how, all drunk with joy, singed by battles' deadly toil
In the black-and-white war footage back they come to their home soil.
Trains are slowly pulling in just as turmoil grows within.
With the brass band getting louder, tears make blind the marching theme.
You are there, one of the mass, spot the two of us at last,
With a scornful short expletive greeting your admiring lads.
In the crowds that block my view is the former, no-one's you,
And she walks away in silence, heading right into her youth.
Well, so be it, I don't mind. All the bad things left behind,
One would hope from this time onwards you are going to be fine.
Back at school in window light come to stand as once you liked.
Hear the maiden name break silence, bringing in the frosty night.

1998

Notes

[1] The archaic demonstrative particle ce means "here is".

[2] Вертаться is a colloquial and dialect word meaning "to return". Like other Ukrainianisms, it tends to be emotionally coloured. The normative Russian equivalent is возвращаться.

[3] A clue to the initials can be found in Gandlevsky's short novel *Трепанация черепа* (*Trepanation*): "Или права была моя почти первая любовь, Ирина Бороздина, что я волшебник, и все, к чему я прикасаюсь, превращается в дерьмо?" (Perhaps my almost first love Irina Borozdina was right all along: I am indeed a magician and everything I touch turns into shit). There seems to be a faint sound of the name Irína Borozdiná at the very end of the original, immediately following the words "Имя, девичью фамилию" (the name and maiden surname); this sound is reproduced in the translation.

[4] A reference to an episode from 'The Tale of Tsar Saltán' by Pushkin where two characters are sealed up in a cask which is then cast into the sea:

> Сын на ножки поднялся́,
> В дно головкой уперся́,
> Понатужился немножко:
> «Как бы здесь на двор окошко
> Нам проделать?» — молвил он,
> Вышиб дно и вышел вон.
>
> •
>
> Murmuring: "I wonder how
> We could break our prison now?"
> Up the son stood on his toes,
> Stretched himself, and said: "Here goes!" –
> Thrust his head against the lid,
> Burst it out – and forth he slid.
>
> (Translated by Louis Zelikoff)

[5] Alexander Soprovsky (1953–1990), a fellow poet who was killed in a traffic accident.

[6] Andropovka is the colloquial name of an inexpensive brand of vodka which was on sale when Yuri Andropov (1914–1984) was the leader of the country: between late 1982 and early 1984. This period detail is a marker of the time warp that occurs in the poem.

[7] The form of this poem does, in fact, resemble a sequence of *chastushki* (частушки, humorous or ironic folk-song miniatures, a kind of Russian doggerel), with little refinement by Gandlevsky's standards. This is likely to be a device used by the poet for conveying raw emotion. *Chastushki* often feature non-normative vocabulary, but in contrast to their English counterparts they can be quite sophisticated formally; their metrical paradigm includes half-length and double-length syllables.

In this case the form is the third paeon, with *aaa* rhyming:

The first two verse lines of each tercet are merged in the typographic arrangement: again, in line with the *chastushki* tradition which requires either two or four lines per stanza.

The poet Boris Slutsky (included in this anthology) was still alive, though no longer writing, at the time of this imagined episode. The reference here is to the "de-poetisation of poetry" characteristic of his style, which was especially prominent in his late works.

The same old heaven

все то же небо

Владимир Вишневский

р. 1953

* * *

А незнакомок я целую робко…

* * *

Я умираю, но об этом — позже…

* * *

Все больше людей нашу тайну хранит…

* * *

О, сколько ты мне, Гордость, позволяла…

* * *

А вот жену здесь расчленять не надо…

Vladimir Vishnevsky

b.1953

* * *

But if a stranger, I would kiss her coyly.

* * *

I'm dying, but we'll talk it over later…

* * *

Our secret is kept by a growing cohort.

* * *

I'm shocked how much, oh Pride, you did permit me…

* * *

Don't come dismembering your wife in here.

Евгений Бунимович

р. 1954

Контрольная работа № 1

А. Кушнеру

Падают доски…
Идет общешкольный ремонт.
Он затянулся, как подобает ремонту.
Я засыпаю во время контрольных работ,
но подавляю, как подобает, зевоту…

Падают листья…
В класс залетает, кружась,
несколько реплик прораба откуда-то сверху.
Школы и жизни осуществляется связь.
В третьей задаче не забывайте проверку.

Осень в России…
В четвертой задаче чертеж
необходим, и, говоря откровенно,
выйдешь из школы — Бог знает, куда забредешь
в хрестоматийной листве по колено.

В пятой задаче пункт А очевидней, чем Б…
Разве отыщешь ответ на таком листопаде,
если доказано, что равносильна судьбе
осень в России…
Звонок.
Соберите тетради.

Evgeny Bunimovich

b.1954

TEST PAPER NO 1

To A. Kushner [1]

Floor boards are falling...
The builders at school make a mess,
shifting the deadline, as they have to do, every morning.
I fall asleep when I invigilate credit tests,
but I suppress, just as I have to do, sighs and yawning.

Red leaves are falling...
Flying right into the class,
building contractors' expletives descend from up there.
School's getting closer again to the laboring mass.
In Question 3 there's a second solution, take care.

Autumn in Russia...
All those who attempt Question 4,
do draw a sketch, but this isn't straightforward:
after the classes who knows just which way one may go,
wading knee-deep across classical foliage.

In Question 5, section B is less easy than A...
Leaf fall. The answers. How could we decide on the right one?
Given the truth that it is tantamount to fate:
autumn in Russia...
The bell.
Everybody, stop writing.

* * *

Год за́ три —
                    поскольку отчасти гоним.
Всегда броневик
                    под всегда воспаленную речь!
И деньги нужны позарез —
                    чтоб их бросить в камин,
и слава нужна позарез —
                    чтобы ей пренебречь...

Я писем длиннее
                    уже никогда не писал
и женщин страшнее
                    уже никогда не любил,[2]
и свет вырубал,[3]
                    и когда его снова врубил —
отсутствием свиста
                    зашелся пустой кинозал.[4]

Прогулочный катер
                    по трубам Неглинной реки,
комедия масок
                    в семейных трусах «будь готов»,
Дисплея Господня
                    ошибка в начале строки
возводится в степень,
                    в квадрат Патриарших прудов.

И слава такая —
                    которой легко пренебречь,
и деньги такие —
                    которые только в камин,
и речи такие —
                    которые до́лжно пресечь,
и годы такие,
                    которые три — за один...

1990

* * *

A year counts as three,
                    since I'm partly oppressed.
An armored car – always,
                    and always a speech that's inflamed! [5]
I'm needy for cash:
                    it would go straight into my fireplace; [6]
I'm needy for fame:
                    it would be disregarded, disdained...

I have never written a letter
                    already as long,[7]
I have never fallen for women
                    already as hard.
I slammed off the lights –
                    and the moment I slam them back on,
the absence of boos
                    wrecks the void of the House of Film Art.

A pleasure craft voyaging
                    through the Neglínnaya pipes.[8]
Commedia dell'arte,
                    the cast in boy-scout underpants.
The typo in God's file,
                    in one of the earlier bytes,
gets raised to a power,
                    the square of the Patriarch Ponds.[9]

The fame, of the kind
                    it would take no heart pain to disdain;
the cash, of the kind
                    that's good only to stoke one's fireplace;
the speeches, from which
                    it is proper and right to restrain;
the years, of which three
                    could have fit in a single one's space...

1990

Notes

1 Alexander Kushner, a poet included in this anthology. Bunimovich has been a teacher of mathematics for over 30 years; Kushner worked as a school teacher (of Russian language and literature) in the 1960s.

2 The first two lines of this stanza have virtually the same, deliberately ambiguous, grammatical structure: the third word of each line can be interpreted either as an adjective qualifying the preceding noun or as an adverb qualifying the verb phrase that follows it. In the first line the competing interpretations yield effectively the same meaning ("I have never written letters at greater length" or "I have never written longer letters"), but in the second line the two meanings are very different, creating a comical ambiguity: "I have never been more frightfully in love with women" or "I have never been in love with more frightful women".

Capturing this quality in translation is a challenge. Tempting though it might be to utilise the habitual confusion between comparative forms of adjectives and adverbs in American colloquial parlance (e.g. "this would be achieved easier" instead of "this would be achieved more easily"), the translator has judged that doing this would lower the tone of the poem without necessarily conveying the playful ambiguity of the original. Instead, the translation provides a hint at this feature by making the corresponding two lines look as if they have the same grammatical structure while actually they do not.

3 Here вырубать means to shut off.

4 Зайтись accompanied by an object in the ablative case means to become completely engrossed in the action expressed by the object.

5 A mocking reference to the political speech made by Lenin from the top of an armoured car on his arrival to St Petersburg in 1917.

6 A reference to an episode from *The Idiot* by Dostoyevsky.

7 The original is deliberately illogical in the use of tense and aspect in this stanza, reflecting the breakdown of time described in the poem. See also note 2 above.

8 Neglinnaya (Неглинная), or Neglinka (Неглинка), is a river in central Moscow which has been running through underground pipes since the 19th century.

[9] A rectangular pond in central Moscow. The pond and the area around it are traditionally referred to in the plural (Патриаршие пруды), as there used to be three interconnected ponds there.

Тимур Кибиров

р. 1955

* * *

В вагоне ночном пассажиры сидят.
Читают они, или пьют, или спят.
И каждый отводит испуганный взгляд.
И каждый во всем виноват.

И что тут сказать, на кого тут пенять.
Уж лучше читать, или пить, или спать.
И каждый мечтает им всем показать
когда-нибудь кузькину мать.

Timur Kibirov

b.1955

* * *

At night on a train men are sitting in rows,
some reading, some drinking, some trying to doze,
and each looks away if he's glanced at up close,
and each feels he's guilty of course.

And what's there to say of this, what is the cause?
It's better to read, or to drink, or to doze.
And each craves a future when courage he draws
for bloodying everyone's nose.

Кризис вышесреднего возраста

Славный бес мне в ребро. Под откос,
кувыркаясь, скорбя и ликуя,
с панталыку сорвавшись, лечу я,[1]
Песню песней горланя всерьез!

Песня песней, а жизнь-то бежит.[2]
Гляну в зеркало — с ужасом вижу —
это что же за клоун бесстыжий
щурит глазки и губы кривит?

И, в зубах папироску зажав,
шутки шутит похабная рожа,
передразнивает так похоже,
что, наверно, он все-таки прав.

AFTER-MIDLIFE CRISIS

What an imp in my rib! Into hell,[3]
tumbling, grieving and feeling triumphant,
I am falling astray, and my anthem
is the Song of Songs – earnestly yelled!

Be the Song of songs, what of this life?
Just a glance in the mirror – shock horror –
who might be this comedian poor,
squinting, pouting, and faking a laugh?

With a fag in the slit of his teeth,
there he jeers, what a twit foul-mouthed,
so believably acting it out
that I think, after all, right he is.

Notes

[1] This is a variation of the idiom "сбить(ся) с панталыку", meaning to lead (to go) astray or to confuse (oneself).

[2] This time "Песня песней" is not only the title of the Song of Songs but also a special phrasal pattern of the Russian language. Two adjacent occurrences of the same noun, the first in the nominative and the second in the ablative case, form a phrase whose meaning is "setting <the noun> aside, ...". Furthermore, only the first word of a title is normally capitalised under the Russian orthographic conventions, which is what enabled the poet to create the intended dual meaning.

[3] The original quotes the second half of the proverb "Седина в бороду, а бес в ребро" (literally, "When a streak of grey gets into your beard, the devil gets into your rib") which refers to middle-aged men's proclivity for much younger women.

Вера Павлова

р. 1963

* * *

Хождение
по водам
замерзшим
на коньках.
Моление о чаше
с бутылкою в руках.
Откуда взяться чаше?
Давайте из горла́.[1]
Каток на Патриарших.[2]
Жизнь, как коньки,
мала.

Vera Pavlova

b.1963

* * *

To walk and walk
on waters,
on frozen ones,
on skates.
To twist the Garden Prayer [3]
may be the least it takes:
Who would a cup purvey us?
Drink from the bottle, dudes.
A rink in Prelate's Square.[4]
Life's tight
as skating boots.

* * *

За пианино, к целому свету спиной.
За пианино, как за высокой стеной.
За пианино, в него уходя, как в забой,
как в запой. Никого не беря с собой.

* * *

Playing the piano – turning one's back to the world.
Playing the piano – buttressed behind a tall wall.
Playing the piano – plunging into a mine vault,
into a drinking bout. Keeping everyone out.

Notes

[1] "Из горла́", with a non-normative stress on the last syllable and often omitting the verb, is an idiom meaning to drink [alcohol] directly from the bottle, which usually happens in an inappropriate place as well. The normative version of this expression would be "пить из горлышка".

[2] See note 9 on p. 333.

[3] 'Walking on the Waters' (Хождение по водам) and 'The Garden Prayer' ('Моление о чаше', literally, "praying about the cup") are established subjects of Russian icons, although some experts are questioning the canonical status of the latter subject, which refers to Mark 14: 36, and consider paintings on this theme religious miniatures rather than true icons.

[4] In the original the location of the skating rink is Patriarch's Ponds in Moscow; this is linked with the earlier religious references.

Константин Кравцов

р. 1963

Сияние

> И изглажу грех земли сей...[1]
>
> Зах. 3, 9

И называлась та земля Яма́л,
но говорить я власти не имел
и имени ее не называл.

Оленьих улиц плыл дощатый мел,
и звездами до дна промерзших вод
дышала ночь, тепла нам не суля.

Лучи водили белый хоровод,
и не имела голоса земля.

Konstantin Kravtsov

b.1963

NORTHERN LIGHTS

> And I will remove the iniquity of that land...
>
> Zech. 3: 9

That land was known to bear the name Yamál,[2]
but I had no authority to speak
and so its name was not for me to call.[3]

Plank-fronted, chalk-stained huts braced reindeer streets;
the stars of waters frozen to their bed
suffused the night's breath. Warmth was not at hand.

Streaks of white light round-dancing overhead,
bereft of voice lay, powerless, the land.[4]

Новогодний натюрморт

Висят две рыбы в сетке за окном
С глазницами, изъеденными солью.

Чешуйки света в воздухе застыли
И зимнее язычество рябины,
И птичьей лапой телебашня замерла,
Продетая в кольцо «Седьмого неба».

В отечестве моем голодных нет,
И нынче даже голуби и галки
Рябину не клюют, роняя снег,
Волнуя невода́ холодных веток.

В отечестве моем голодных нет,
И делят пустошь снега вместо хлеба
Пророки, что не явлены на свет
По крохам собирать всё то же небо.

Помилуй мя, где в извести часы [5]
Остановили стрелки на одних
И тех же цифрах в желтых коридорах,
Где ветви, телебашни, рыбы спят,
Соль в пустошах
            глазниц и циферблатов.

1988, общежитие Литинститута

Konstantin Kravtsov

STILL LIFE ON CHRISTMAS DAY [6]

Two fish hang off the window in a net,
With their eye sockets by rock salt eroded.[7]

With scales of light suspended in the air,
Next to a winter rowan's pagan worship
The bird-leg TV tower is transfixed,
Squeeze-banded by the ring of Seventh Heaven.[8]

No-one is starving in my fatherland,
And even doves and jackdaws, being too sated
For rowan berries, do not drop the snow
Or wave the nets of cold and tangled branches.

No-one is starving in my fatherland.[9]
Not bread, the void of snow is being shared
By prophets of the kind that are not sent
To gather, crumb by crumb, the same old heaven.

Have mercy, Lord, upon me, where paint-stained
Clocks hold their hands still, and display the same
Time everywhere along stretched yellow hallways,
And where all towers, fish, and branches sleep
While salt fills up the voids
                              of dials and sockets.

1988, The Literary Institute, Students' Residence

Notes

[1] Here, сей is the genitive case of the archaic feminine demonstrative pronoun сия: "of this [land]". The modern Russian equivalent is эта (nominative), этой (genitive).

[2] The Yamal peninsula in Western Siberia, beyond the Arctic Circle. The name means "the land's end" in the language of its Nenets inhabitants. This unexpected turn of the epigraph can be seen as alluding to the history of the Gulag camps in the area: on one of the semantic layers, Kravtsov is interpreting northern lights as a sign that God has not forsaken the Russian North despite the apparent evidence to the contrary.

[3] An allusion to Gen. 2: 19–20 where Adam gives names to all cattle, fowl and beasts (and according to the Orthodox tradition, becomes their master by virtue of that). It may also be a reference to poetic gift as being a divine authority to speak. At both levels the narrator is not yet able to see the true nature of things and therefore to name them and to acquire power over them.

[4] At the sight of the lights, all things material ("land" and "earth" are the same word in Russian) lose, in turn, their authority to speak and hence their power over the narrator. This aspect of the intended meaning, explained by the author in a private communication, has been strengthened in translation.

The aurora borealis is an important motif in Kravtsov's poetry, both as a natural phenomenon characteristic of his native North and as a symbol of spiritual values. The author is an Orthodox priest.

[5] Мя is an archaic, and Church Slavonic, form of меня (the accusative case of the first-person singular pronoun: "me"). The formula "помилуй мя" corresponds to the Catholic "miserere mei" and can be used either in prayers or idiomatically even by Russian speakers unfamiliar with Church Slavonic.

[6] The literal meaning of the title is 'A New-Year Still Life', but this poem has also been published with the title 'Christmas 1988'. Orthodox Christmas is on January 7.

[7] Salt-cured fish, likely to be the Caspian roach (вобла, *Rutilus rutilus caspicus*), which in Russia is customarily consumed as an accompaniment to beer. A string bag, colloquially referred to as сетка (net),

suspended outside a window is a common substitute for a fridge/freezer.

The combination of fish and a net-like string bag starts a chain of Christian symbols which continues throughout the poem. For the meaning of salt, with references to which this poem begins and ends, see note 10 on p. 45. The New Testament symbolism of salt as something which preserves from corruption (Matt. 5: 13, Col. 4: 6) may also be relevant here.

[8] The ring-shaped revolving restaurant located at a height of 334 metres up the Ostankino TV tower in Moscow.

[9] The second occurrence of this line (which opens two consecutive stanzas) refers to spiritual, rather than physical, hunger. Nobody wants the fish, neither as food nor as a symbol.

This stanza is rhymed (*aBaB*) in the generally unrhymed original. It is not clear whether this was intentional, but weak sonorities were introduced in the translation just in case.

Борис Рыжий

1974—2001

* * *

Довольно я поездил в поездах,
не меньше полетал на самолетах.
Соль жизни в постоянных поворотах,
всё остальное тлен, вернее прах.[1]
Купе. Блондинка двадцати двух лет
глядит в окно, изрядно беспокоясь:
когда мы часовой проедем пояс,
то сразу потемнеет или нет?
Который час я на нее смотрю,
хотя упорно не смотреть стараюсь.
А тут обмяк, открыто улыбаюсь:
— А как же, дорогуша! — говорю.

Boris Ryzhy

1974–2001

* * *

I've had my share of trips by long-haul train
and I have been on quite a few airliners.
Life's all about a change and realignment,
and all the rest is for the grave to claim.
A train compartment. A mid-twenties blonde
keeps looking out the window, really fussing:
when we approach the point of time-zone crossing,
will it grow dark immediately or not?
I've looked at her while keeping up my guard,
I have been looking furtively for hours.
But this time, feeling more at ease and roused,
I utter with a smile: "You bet, sweetheart!"

Мщение Ахилла

Издевайся как хочешь, кощунствуй, Ахилл,
    ты сильней и хитрей, мчи его вокруг Трои.
Прав ли, нет ли, безумец, но ты победил —
    это первое, а правота — лишь второе.
Пусть тебя не простят, но и ты не простил.

Пусть за телом притащится старый Приам.
    Но отдав, не в содеянном ты усомнишься.
Ты герой, ты не крови боишься из ран —
    чужды слезы героям, и слез ты боишься,
хоть и плакал не раз, обращаясь к богам.

Не за то ли ты с жизнью-уродкой «на ты»,
    что однажды «на ты» был со смертью-красоткой?
...Ночь целует убитых в открытые рты,
    голубые, пропахшие греческой водкой,
и созвездья у них в головах — как цветы...

Achilles's Revenge

Oh Achilles, ride on, desecrate and blaspheme.
    You are tougher and smarter, drag him over potholes.
Right or wrong, madman, yes: there's no doubt that you win.
    That's the thing; being right isn't half as important.
You may not get forgiveness, but none was for him.

Let the body be claimed by old Priam on foot.
    You'll release it, but not since your heart is unclear.
You're a hero, so warriors' blood is your loot –
    heroes aren't used to tears, and it's tears that you fear,
though you've shed them in prayers when nobody looked.

Aren't you acting familiar with Life – a vile louse –
    just because beauty Death was once also familiar?
...Night is kissing the fallen on their open mouths –
    blue ones, reeking of foul Grecian vodka; a million
stars in bright constellations adorn them like flowers.

Notes

1 Тлен is an archaic noun related to тление (decay, putrefaction) and denoting the result rather than the process. Its use in modern Russian is almost universally figurative; the word mainly occurs in expressions such as "тлен и прах" (ashes and dust).

Appendix

Russian History of the 20th Century:
a Timeline

1903   The Trans-Siberian railway is completed.

1904   War with Japan begins.

1905   The Bloody Sunday massacre in St Petersburg.

        The war with Japan ends. Japan gains control of Korea,
        southern Manchuria and the southern part of Sakhalin.

        A general strike.

        A massive anti-Jewish pogrom in Odessa.

1906   The first *Duma* (parliament) is convened and shortly
        dissolved.

        An agrarian reform is introduced by Prime Minister Stolypin.

1911   Student disorders.

        Stolypin is assassinated.

1912   The Lena goldfield massacre.

1913   Three hundred years' anniversary of the Romanov dynasty.

1914   World War I begins. St Petersburg is renamed Petrograd.

1916   A major offensive against Austro-Hungarians in Galicia (west
        Ukraine).

        Rasputin is murdered in an attempt to save the monarchy.

1917   A Provisional Government is set up.

        Tsar Nicholas II abdicates.

        The October Revolution. The Bolsheviks, led by Lenin, seize
        power.

        Armistice is declared on the German front.

Finland gains independence.

Cheka (the secret police) is set up.

1918   Russia withdraws from World War I.

The capital is moved from Petrograd to Moscow.

The Civil War and the Allied intervention begin.

Lithuania, Estonia, Latvia, Ukraine, Armenia, Azerbaijan and Georgia declare independence.

Tsar Nicholas II is executed along with other members of his immediate family.

Red Terror is declared.

1919   War with Poland begins.

1920   Soviet power is established in Azerbaijan and Armenia.

1921   The Volga basin famine begins.

Strikes in Petrograd and Moscow. The Kronstadt rebellion.

The war with Poland ends. The border is negotiated; Ukraine is partitioned.

Soviet power is installed in Georgia.

The New Economic Policy is declared.

1922   The Civil War ends.

The Volga famine ends.

The USSR is created.

1923   The ailing Lenin is removed from public life.

Stalin's rise to power begins.

1924   Lenin dies. Petrograd is renamed Leningrad.

1927   The 15th Party Congress. Stalin's grip on power is consolidated.

1928   The Shakhty Trial (the first of the show trials).

The first Five Year Plan is introduced.

1929   Forced collectivisation begins.

1930   The Gulag system is established.

1932   The Southern famine crisis begins.

The second Five Year plan begins.

All literary groups are dismantled and the Union of Soviet Writers is created.

Stalin's wife commits suicide.

1933   The Southern famine ends. The death toll runs into millions.

1934   OGPU (the successor of *Cheka*) is incorporated into NKVD.

The First congress of the Union of Soviet Writers.

Kirov, seen by some as a possible challenger to Stalin, is assassinated.

1936   A purge of former Left Bolsheviks.

Show trials.

The "Stalin Constitution" is promulgated.

1937   A purge of the Army.

Eight military leaders are arrested, tried and executed; the ninth accused commits suicide to avoid arrest.

Show trials.

Mass terror begins.

1938   A purge of Right Bolsheviks.

Show trials.

1939   The Red Army defeats the Japanese at Khalkin-Gol in Mongolia.

The Treaty of Non-Aggression with Germany is signed.

World War II begins.

Western Ukraine and Western Byelorussia are annexed.

The Winter War with Finland begins. The USSR is expelled from the League of Nations.

1940   The Winter War ends. Finland loses some territory but retains its sovereignty.

The Baltic States and Bessarabia are annexed.

Unjustifiable absence from work is made a criminal offence.

1941   Germany invades the USSR.

The Siege of Leningrad begins.

The German army is thrown back from Moscow.

1942   The German army launches a major offensive in southern Russia.

1943   Victory in the Battle of Stalingrad. The tide of the war turns in favour of the USSR.

The Teheran Conference between Stalin, Roosevelt and Churchill.

A separate NKGB (state security) is established alongside NKVD (domestic affairs).

1944   The Red Army advances to Poland and Romania.

The Siege of Leningrad ends.

Deportation of the entire Chechen, Ingush, Kalmyk, Balkar, Karachay, Meskhetian Turkish and Crimean Tatar populations.

1945   Germany surrenders.

The US drops atomic bombs on Hiroshima and Nagasaki.

The USSR enters the war against Japan.

World War II ends. The USSR losses are estimated between 20 and 30 million dead.

1946   A famine begins in Ukraine.

The "Iron Curtain" speech by Churchill.

1947	The Ukrainian famine ends.
1948	An anti-Jewish campaign.
	The blockade of West Berlin begins.
1949	Purges of East European Communist Parties.
	NATO is formed.
	The Berlin Blockade ends.
	The USSR conducts a successful test of an atomic bomb.
1950	The Korean War begins.
1953	The Doctors' Plot: an alleged large-scale conspiracy to poison top Soviet leaders.
	Stalin dies. Khrushchev comes to power.
	Those arrested in connection with the Doctors' Plot are acquitted.
	Uprising in East Germany.
	The Korean War ends.
1954	Khrushchev begins to release political prisoners and close down the camps.
	KGB is set up as a successor of MGB (formerly NKGB) and NKVD.
1955	The Warsaw Pact is established.
1956	Khrushchev denounces Stalin in the "Secret Speech" at the 20th Party Congress.
	Riots in Poland.
	The Hungarian Revolution is suppressed through Soviet intervention. Thousands die.
1957	The USSR launches the first satellite, Sputnik.
	The 6th World Festival of Youth and Students is held in Moscow, becoming a symbol of Khruschev's "thaw".
1959	Castro seizes power in Cuba.

1960	Diplomatic conflict with China intensifies. The USSR ends its economic and military aid.
	An American high-altitude spy plane, flown from a base in Pakistan, is shot down near Sverdlovsk; the pilot is captured.
	The Paris Summit between Eisenhower and Khrushchev collapses.
1961	Construction of the Berlin Wall begins.
	Castro declares that Cuba is to adopt communism.
	Yuri Gagarin orbits the Earth. The USSR consolidates its leadership in the Space Race.
1962	The Cuban Missile Crisis. The USSR withdraws missiles from Cuba.
1964	Khrushchev is deposed. Brezhnev becomes the leader of the Communist Party.
1965	Major oil fields are discovered in Western Siberia.
1967	The USSR severs diplomatic relations with Israel.
1968	Prague Spring is suppressed by Warsaw Pact troops.
1969	A border conflict with China. War is narrowly avoided.
	The Apollo 11 mission. The USSR loses the race to the Moon.
1970	The economy slows down and enters a prolonged period of stagnation.
1974	The USSR becomes the world's largest oil producer.
1979	Soviet intervention in Afghanistan begins.
1980	The Solidarity movement is founded in Poland.
1982	Brezhnev dies. Andropov (a former head of KGB) comes to power.
1983	Cold War tensions increase.
	A Korean Boeing 747 strays over the USSR and is shot down.
1984	Pershing missiles are deployed in Western Europe by the US.

1985	Gorbachev comes to power following the deaths of Andropov and Chernenko.
	Gromyko is replaced as Minister of Foreign Affairs after 28 years in the job.
	An anti-alcohol campaign.
1986	The Chernobyl nuclear disaster.
	Riots in Kazakhstan.
1987	Political and economic reforms.
	Matthias Rust lands his plane in central Moscow. Personnel changes in the Soviet Army.
1988	The territorial conflict between Armenia and Azerbaijan turns violent.
1989	The USSR withdraws its troops from Afghanistan.
	A violent crackdown of the nationalist demonstration in Tbilisi, Georgia.
	The Berlin Wall comes down.
	The collapse of communism in Eastern Europe.
1990	Lithuania and Latvia declare independence.
	Germany is reunited.
1991	Yeltsin is elected President of the Russian Federation within the USSR.
	An attempted coup by hardliners in the USSR government. Yeltsin leads the resistance.
	Leningrad is renamed St Petersburg.
	Estonia declares independence.
	Diplomatic relations with Israel are restored.
	The Warsaw Pact is dissolved.
	The USSR is dissolved.

1993   The constitutional crisis.

        Russia is on the brink of civil war.

1994   Russian troops enter separatist Chechnya.

1996   Ceasefire in Chechnya. Withdrawal of the Russian troops is
        agreed.

1998   A financial crisis leads to devaluation of the rouble.

1999   A series of apartment-block bombings in Moscow.

        Russian forces are re-deployed in Chechnya.

2000   Putin is elected President.

Looking Up Samples

Не мог он ямба от хорея,
Как мы ни бились, отличить.

•

Do what we would, he took forever
Iambic for trochaic verse.

Alexander Pushkin
(translated by Walter Arndt)

The Metre and Rhyme-Scheme Finders that follow this section help to locate samples of poems written in a particular form. All complete Russian poems occurring anywhere in the book are included in the indexes. The translation of each sample (or, in one case, of the German original whose Russian translation is indexed) can be found either on the facing page or in the surrounding text.

Determining the metre and rhyme scheme may involve subjective judgement, although ambiguities are relatively rare. The following considerations are important:

- Verse lines do not always coincide with typographic lines. Rhymes provide a more reliable indication of verse line ends.
- Similarly, the number of verse lines in the rhyme scheme may differ from the number of verse lines in the stanza. However, the stanzaic form is not irrelevant, and may play a role in determining the rhyme scheme of the poem: for example, in distinguishing *aa* from *aabb*.

Metres are classified by verse form and syllabic-accentual foot type, with the subentries being based on the number of feet or beats per verse line. So, for instance, the place to look for samples of iambic tetrameter would be the subentry "tetrameter" under the header "iamb" in the Metre Finder. The subentry "mixed" under a metre header indicates that a stable stanzaic pattern is formed by lines of different length: for example, 4-2-4-2; "variable" means that the length of verse lines varies freely while the metrical type stays the same.

The primary classification of rhyme schemes is by size: the number of verse lines in the recurring rhyme pattern. Subentries in the Rhyme Scheme Finder represent specific rhyme schemes denoted using the symbols defined on p. xvii: for example, *aaBccB* and *AbAbAb* are both found under the header "6 lines". The subentry "mixed" under a size header describes a combination of different rhyme patterns of the same size supported by a stable number of lines per typographic stanza: for example, when a poem mixes *aBaB* and *AbbA* quatrains. Rhyming arrangements that combine patterns of different size (e.g. *AA* and *AbAb*), or those not based on any recurring pattern, are classified as "special".

Occasional deviations from a generally stable metre or rhyme scheme are ignored for the purposes of classification and indexing.

Metre Finder

accentual
  3-beat 342
  4-beat 54, 152, 170

amphibrach
  mixed 80, 164, 168, 334
  pentameter 18, 330
  tetrameter 248, 280, 326
  trimeter 128, 284

anapaest
  mixed 10, 288, 300
  pentameter 148
  tetrameter xxxix, 74, 222, 354
  trimeter 226, 228, 254, 336
  variable 102

dactyl
  dimeter 46
  pentameter 306, 328
  tetrameter 92, 182, 212
  variable 186

dolnik
  3-beat 158
  4-beat 12, 126, 268

elegiac distich 240, 242

iamb
  hexameter 26, 40, 192, 292
  mixed 14, 28, 36, 48, 172

  pentameter 4, 8, 66, 88, 96, 98, 196, 220, 230, 238, 264, 272, 294, 296, 312, 326, 346, 348, 352
  tetrameter 24, 30, 52, 72, 78, 100, 138, 146, 154, 156, 200, 208, 274, 318
  trimeter 340
  variable 108, 282

idiosyncratic 106, 132, 134, 204, 206, 260

logaoedic
  3-foot 112, 114, 244
  4-foot 302
  5-foot 308
  6-foot 82, 252
  mixed 258, 290

paeon 3rd
  mixed 320
  trimeter 6

trochee
  hexameter 68, 216
  mixed 140
  octameter 178
  pentameter 20, 34, 42, 122, 285, 314
  tetrameter 86, 120, 162, 174, 232, 322

See p. 366 for explanations.

Appendix

Rhyme Scheme Finder

2 lines
  aa xxxix, 6, 26, 92, 158, 285, 296
  AA 68, 216
  αα 186

3 lines
  aaa 320

4 lines
  aaaa 334
  aabb 74, 268
  abab 12, 18, 28, 80, 112, 330, 346
  aBaB 4, 14, 36, 42, 168, 292, 328
  AbAb 10, 34, 46, 66, 82, 100, 102, 120, 140, 154, 162, 164, 174, 178, 182, 244, 314, 318
  A'bA'b 200
  ABAB 20, 114, 212, 252, 280, 302
  A'BA'B 122
  aB'aB' 48, 258
  aBBa 86, 238, 336, 352
  AβAβ 52
  mixed 72, 126, 128, 138, 192, 208, 220, 272, 284, 306

αβαβ 54, 156
αββα 40

5 lines
  ababa 170
  aBaBa 354
  Xabba 172

6 lines
  aabccb 290
  aaBccB 98, 226, 288, 308
  AAbCCb 228, 230
  AbAbAb 254
  mixed 264

8 lines
  AAAbCCCb 196
  xA'xbxA'xb 260

interlocking rubaiyat
  aaba bbab 222

sonnet
  aBBa aBBa CCd EEd 30

special 24, 78, 88, 106, 108, 132, 134, 146, 148, 152, 204, 206, 232, 248, 274, 282, 300, 340, 342

unrhymed 8, 96, 240, 242, 294, 312, 348

See p. 366 for explanations and p. xvii for the meaning of the symbols.

Index of Poets

Алфавитный список авторов

Lightning Source UK Ltd.
Milton Keynes UK
26 October 2009

145396UK00002B/2/P